MW01383200

355 Transforming the warfare state; global militarism
Tra   and economic conversion. Hudson, WI: Gary E.
    McCuen Publications, Inc., 1992.
    155p. (Ideas in Conflict Series)

1.Militarism 2.Military--Appropriations & expenditures
3.Economic conversion

Transforming the WARFARE STATE

Global Militarism and Economic Conversion

Gary E. McCuen

IDEAS IN CONFLICT SERIES

SOUTHFIELD CHRISTIAN SCHOOL LIBRARY

502 Second Street
Hudson, Wisconsin 54016
Phone (715) 386-7113

All rights reserved. No part of this book may be reproduced or stored by any means without prior permission from the copyright owner.

Illustrations & Photo Credits

Blashko 107, Carol*Simpson 27, 54, 81 N. Goldberg 122, 142 Ollie Harrington 37, 69 S. Joseph 15, 41 Office of Technology Assessment 10, 22 Steve Sack 60, 95 U.S. Arms Control and Disarmament Agency 114 U.S. Department of Defense 33, 77, 87, 102, 129 Richard Wright 48. Cover illustration by Ron Swanson.

©1992 by Gary E. McCuen Publications, Inc.
502 Second Street, Hudson, Wisconsin 54016

(715) 386-7113

International Standard Book Number
0-86596-083-6 Printed in the United States of America

CONTENTS

Ideas in Conflict   6

1. WORLD MILITARY SPENDING: 8
EDITOR'S OVERVIEW
Gary E. McCuen

CHAPTER 1 THE MILITARY ROLE IN A CHANGING WORLD

2. THE WARFARE STATE MUST   13
BE DISMANTLED
William W. Winpisinger

3. THE WORLD IS STILL A DANGEROUS PLACE   20
Harold Brown

4. MILITARY SPENDING LEVELS ARE   25
NOT SUSTAINABLE
Robert S. McNamara

5. DEFENSE SPENDING MUST BE MAINTAINED   31
C. A. McKinney

CHAPTER 2 ECONOMIC CONVERSION: SWORDS INTO PLOWSHARES

6. ECONOMIC CONVERSION NEEDS   39
GOVERNMENT DIRECTION
Jonathan Feldman

7. GOVERNMENT PLANNING   46
WILL NOT WORK
William Poole

8. ECONOMIC CONVERSION WILL PROMOTE   52
PEACE AND JUSTICE
Amata Miller

9. ECONOMIC CONVERSION HAS BEEN   58
A FAILURE
U.S. Arms Control Annual Report

CHAPTER 3 MILITARY SPENDING AND SOCIAL NEEDS

10. MILITARISM DEPLETES THE CIVILIAN ECONOMY
    David Alexander — 67

11. MILITARY SPENDING DOES NOT HURT OUR ECONOMY
    Richard Cheney — 74

12. THE ARMS RACE HAS CRIPPLED SOCIAL PROGRAMS
    The Congressional Black Caucus — 79

13. DOMESTIC SPENDING, NOT DEFENSE, IS THE CULPRIT
    M. Stanton Evans — 85

CHAPTER 4 GLOBAL MILITARISM

14. NON-VIOLENCE IS THE WAY TO PEACE
    The War Resisters League — 93

15. VIOLENCE CAN BE A NECESSARY EVIL
    John Garvey — 100

16. STOPPING THE WAR AGAINST THE THIRD WORLD
    Michael T. Klare — 105

17. PREPARING TO WIN LOW-INTENSITY CONFLICTS
    David Silverstein — 112

18. A NEW MILITARY BUDGET FOR A NEW WORLD
    The Center for Defense Information — 120

19. THE HIGH COST OF ARMS REDUCTION 127
   Malcolm Wallup

20. IMPOVERISHED BY RUNAWAY 132
   ARMS RACE
   Christian Social Action

21. THIS IS NO TIME TO BEAT OUR SWORDS 136
   INTO PLOWSHARES
   Thomas Sowell

22. EXPOSING THE ROOTS OF MILITARISM 140
   Roger Powers

23. LIVING IN A DANGEROUS WORLD 146
   A. M. Gray

Bibliography 153

REASONING SKILL DEVELOPMENT

These activities may be used as individualized study guides for students in libraries and resource centers or as discussion catalysts in small group and classroom discussions.

1. *Interpreting Editorial Cartoons* 36

2. *What Is Political Bias?* 64

3. *Examining Counterpoints* 90

4. *What Is Editorial Bias?* 151

This series features ideas in conflict on political, social, and moral issues. It presents counterpoints, debates, opinions, commentary, and analysis for use in libraries and classrooms. Each title in the series uses one or more of the following basic elements:

Introductions that present an issue overview giving historic background and/or a description of the controversy.

Counterpoints and debates carefully chosen from publications, books, and position papers on the political right and left to help librarians and teachers respond to requests that treatment of public issues be fair and balanced.

Symposiums and forums that go beyond debates that can polarize and oversimplify. These present commentary from across the political spectrum that reflect how complex issues attract many shades of opinion.

A **global** emphasis with foreign perspectives and surveys on various moral questions and political issues that will help readers to place subject matter in a less culture-bound and ethnocentric frame of reference. In an ever-shrinking and interdependent world, understanding and cooperation are essential. Many issues are global in nature and can be effectively dealt with only by common efforts and international understanding.

Reasoning skill study guides and discussion activities provide ready-made tools for helping with critical reading and evaluation of content. The guides and activities deal with one or more of the following:

RECOGNIZING AUTHOR'S POINT OF VIEW

INTERPRETING EDITORIAL CARTOONS

VALUES IN CONFLICT

WHAT IS EDITORIAL BIAS?

WHAT IS SEX BIAS?

WHAT IS POLITICAL BIAS?

WHAT IS ETHNOCENTRIC BIAS?

WHAT IS RACE BIAS?

WHAT IS RELIGIOUS BIAS?

*From across **the political spectrum** varied sources are presented for research projects and classroom discussions. Diverse opinions in the series come from magazines, newspapers, syndicated columnists, books, political speeches, foreign nations, and position papers by corporations and nonprofit institutions.*

About the Editor

Gary E. McCuen is an editor and publisher of anthologies for public libraries and curriculum materials for schools. Over the past years his publications have specialized in social, moral and political conflict. They include books, pamphlets, cassettes, tabloids, filmstrips and simulation games, many of them designed from his curriculums during 11 years of teaching junior and senior high school social studies. At present he is the editor and publisher of the *Ideas in Conflict* series and the *Editorial Forum* series.

READING

1

WORLD MILITARY SPENDING: EDITOR'S OVERVIEW

Gary E. McCuen

Global military spending during the 1980s reached nearly one trillion dollars (one thousand billion) per year. In 1988 the rich or developed countries invested over 800 billion dollars and the poor nations spent over 170 billion dollars on military acquisitions. The world now has a stockpile of 51,000 nuclear weapons.[1] Many observers believe that neither the global economy nor the planet's basic environmental life support system can long survive the expenditure of money, intellectual effort and productive capacity on this level of war preparation. President Bush proposed a 1992 military budget of nearly 300 billion dollars. Price tags on new weapons systems requested recently would cost over 500 billion dollars:[2] Some examples are listed below.

- Bradley Fighting Vehicle System. An Army personnel carrier. ($12 billion)
- B-2 Stealth Bomber. For fighting a nuclear war with the Soviet Union. ($72 billion)
- New aircraft carriers. The Department of Defense (DOD) wants two more nuclear powered aircraft carriers. (Each new carrier task force costs $18 billion)
- MX ICBM. Intercontinental ballistic missile for fighting a nuclear war with the Soviet Union. ($23.4 billion)
- Division Air Defense (DIVAD) Gun. An Anti-air cannon. (Cancelled after $1.8 billion was spent on it)
- Midgetman ICBM. With 12,000 strategic weapons. ($28 billion)
- Strategic Defense Initiative. A project to develop a shield against nuclear attack. (A total of $21 billion has been spent between fiscal years 1984 and 1990)
- Anti-Satellite Weapons (ASAT). The Pentagon wanted to develop a weapon to destroy Soviet satellites. ($94.5 billion was requested in FY 1990)

- F-14D. A naval aircraft Congress insisted on buying more of, against the Pentagon's wishes. ($1.1 billion for fiscal year 1990)

Seymour Melman, a long time advocate of arms reductions, claims that the U.S. military industrial complex employs 6.5 million civilian and military personnel in more than 135,000 factories, laboratories and bases. He says that "from 1947 to 1989 this country diverted to military purposes resources whose value exceeded the fixed reproducible, tangible wealth of the entire civilian economy. Tens of thousands of factories became virtual wards of the Pentagon; sheltered from the discipline of the marketplace, they adopted inefficient and costly methods. An indirect consequence of the larger share of tax dollars funneled into the military establishment was a diminished public investment in the infrastructure and its resulting decay."[3]

Robert Cwiklik writing in *The Nation* magazine says the real amount of the 1990 military budget balloons from $296.3 billion to $458 billion if other military-related items are included: for example, in 1990 $6.3 billion for strategic planning, $1.2 billion for NASA, and $129 billion for the military's share of the interest on the national debt should be included. This amounts to 50 percent of the 1990 budget if all trust funds are subtracted. [4]

Global Arms Sales

The amount of money nations spent buying and selling arms exceeded just over 60 billion dollars a year in the late 1980s. The poor nations buy arms largely from the rich nations that produce them. Much of the money poor nations use to purchase arms comes from loans, credits and foreign aid from the same developed nations that manufacture most weapons.[5] One serious world dilemma is the development of nuclear capabilities in poor nations. Brazil, India, Pakistan, Iraq, and North Korea are trying to attain nuclear weapons capabilities.

Global Inequity and Environmental Disasters

This enormous military spending looks increasingly untenable in the face of present global economic and environmental problems. The international economic order is a disaster. Over one billion of the earth's five billion live in poverty and despair. Fewer and fewer people are becoming richer and more and more are becoming poorer. In the Horn of Africa, for example, war and conflict have destroyed much of the environment and the ability of people to even feed themselves. The Horn is a great region about the size of half the continental United States.

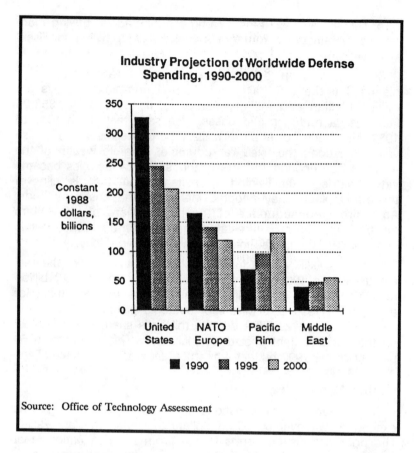

Source: Office of Technology Assessment

Between 19 and 26 million people are either hungry or close to starvation. Economic horror stories like this can be repeated in other great regions of the developing nations. And millions of people live in dire straits within the rich nations of the world. Hunger victimizes 20 million people in the United States and over one billion people worldwide.[6] Third World debt to the rich nations approaches one thousand billion dollars. In 1990 there was a transfer of 50 billion dollars from poor nations to the rich nations to service the interest on this debt [7]. The local and global economic systems promote increasing poverty, disease and economic disintegration in rich and poor nations alike.

The Environment and a Healthy Planet

The economic success of the planet's wealthy few and the endemic global militarism and war have caused havoc with the environment. The earth's ozone layer is being depleted at alarming rates by industrial chemicals. Without this protective layer human life will cease to exist. The world's farmlands are rapidly disappearing with wasteful and destructive agricultural practices in rich and poor nations alike. Lester R. Brown of *World Watch* estimates the world loses 24 billion tons of topsoil each year, and it has lost 480 billion tons in the last 20 years. The world's rainforests are also under threat of extinction and could be gone by the year 2000, and with them half of the living species on the planet. [8]

In his yearly State of the World reports on the environment, Lester Brown points out the following: "Economic growth is creating ecological disaster. Gross world product has grown from $600 billion in 1900 to more than $13 trillion by 1986. World population growth, from 5 billion in 1986 to 6 billion plus by 2000, will create a need for 33 percent more food over the next 13 years. The added strain of that economic activity may well break the world's fragile ecosystem."[9]

In the United States Congress, the Harvest of Peace Resolution proposes changing budget priorities. It calls for a reduction of world military spending by half before the year 2000. The money saved from the reduction could be directed toward saving the poor and saving the planet from ecological destruction. This book examines and debates the methods and wisdom of transforming military production into peaceful activities.

[1]Ruth Leger Sivard, "World Military and Social Expedition", 1991, *World Priorities, Inc.* 1991, pp. 7, 11.

[2]*The Defense Monitor*, "Wasteful Weapons", Vol. 18, number 7, 1989.

[3.]Seymour Melman and Lloyd J. Dumas, "Planning for Economic Conversion", *The Nation*, April 16, 1990, p. 524.

[4]Robert Cwiklik, Ibid., p. 524.

[5]Office of Technology Assessment, *Global Arms Trade*, 1991, pp. 5, 6.

[6] *Christian Social Action*, "Share the Harvest of Peace", May, 1990, p. 15.

[7] Ruth Leger Sivard, Ibid., p. 33.

[8] Ibid, p. 5, 29, 30.

[9] Rod Grub, "Report Says Growth Threatens the Globe", *Minneapolis Star Tribune*, August, 1987.

CHAPTER 1

THE MILITARY ROLE IN A CHANGING WORLD

2. THE WARFARE STATE MUST BE DISMANTLED 13

   William W. Winpisinger

3. THE WORLD IS STILL A DANGEROUS PLACE 20

   Harold Brown

4. MILITARY SPENDING LEVELS ARE NOT SUSTAINABLE 25

   Robert S. McNamara

5. DEFENSE SPENDING MUST BE MAINTAINED 31

   C. A. McKinney

READING

2

THE MILITARY ROLE IN A CHANGING WORLD

THE WARFARE STATE MUST BE DISMANTLED

William W. Winpisinger

William W. Winpisinger is the International President of the International Association of Machinists and Aerospace Workers (IAM).

Points to Consider:

1. Why does the author feel that military contractor employers owe restitution to displaced workers?

2. How would this restitution policy work?

3. What does the author think of military spending as a source of jobs?

4. Describe some of the potential conversions projects. Can you think of any such projects in your own state?

Excerpted from testimony by William W. Winpisinger before the House Subcommittee on Economic Stabilization, June 29, 1988.

Now the truth is that military budget and military spending should never be determined by the number of jobs it will provide. Hitler, Tojo and Mussolini all promised jobs and full employment via military buildup.

We taxpayers and defense workers alike have been betrayed by a corrupt Warfare State and its pseudo-patriotic army of "beltway bandits," conniving consultants, and "defense junkies."

During these past seven years of the military spending spree, we in the International Association of Machinists and Aerospace Workers (IAM) have experienced and witnessed displacement from our jobs by an invasion of expensive new technologies designed to create Orwellian "workerless factories"; we have been stranded on the barren beaches of unemployment while our military contractor employers sailed off to anti-democratic countries or to unfair trading "partners," and set up shop and military manufacturing centers over there, only to increase profits, exploit human and labor rights and make our national defense dependent upon logistically indefensible foreign suppliers.

While this has been going on, our military contractor employers, awash in Pentagon cash and unlimited profits since the Vinson-Trammel Profit Limitation Act was effectively repealed in dark-of-night hearings seven or eight years ago. They have had the unmitigated gall to demand wage and life support benefit concessions from us; demand divisive and unfair two-tier wage schemes; give-up cost-of-living adjustments; and force us on dozens of occasions to take to the streets on strike to preserve the integrity of our collective bargaining contracts and, ultimately, to preserve our union as a free and democratic institution itself.

Restitution

Along with irate citizen taxpayers, we in the IAM demand restitution from those mercenary freebooters, who have used the so-called Defense Budget as their own private slush fund and made the Pentagon the site of a colossal raffle.

Restitution can begin with legislation for Economic Conversion. The Defense Economic Adjustment Act would establish a Workers' Economic Adjustment Reserve Trust Fund in the Treasury Department—a civilian agency. Money for the Fund would come from military contractors themselves. Each contractor would be required to pay 1.25 percent of the gross

value of its contracts into the fund each year. Award of any contract by the Federal Government would be contingent upon that payment into the Workers' Economic Adjustment Fund.

Assuming the Federal Government awards military contracts at the rate of $160 billion a year, a reasonable estimate, then that 1.25 percent payment would put $2 billion a year into the Fund.

That's restitution. And that is a small price for contractors to pay for the system they have so badly abused and misused over the past decade or longer.

Economic Conversion and Jobs

Let's get to Economic Conversion itself. Here's the definition we use in the Machinists Union: Whenever, wherever and for whatever reason military production, whether for goods or services, ceases, then a plan for alternative civilian production will automatically go into effect to make jobless workers and

USELESS WEAPONS

With the military threat from Soviet communism collapsing, is it too much to hope that we might have a little domestic perestroika *and* glasnost? *A first target could be the myths used to justify development and production of 20,000 U.S. tactical nuclear weapons of varied types and sizes, supposedly to fight a nuclear war in Europe.*

An honest discussion would expose the irrationality of what passed as serious thought on nuclear strategy during the past 40 years. It also might put the brakes on spending additional billions to develop newer versions of these useless weapons.

Walter Pincus, **Washington Post,** May 15, 1990

---

impacted communities economically viable and whole.

When military production goes into a community, or a military base is located in a community, then those local communities and school districts receive special federal assistance to help pay for additional public services caused by that military production.

But when that military activity ceases or is taken out of that community, then the workers and the community are left to the fates of unemployment compensation and the free market. The Pentagon does have an Office of Economic Adjustment, but its activity is confined to military base shutdowns.

Over the long run, the military contracting business has been characterized by boom and bust cycles of employment. Projections into the future, even at current excessive levels of military spending, show little or no gains in employment, due primarily to the introduction of labor-displacing technologies on a fairly massive scale, particularly in assembly work and metal cutting and shaping work. Off-shore procurement, that is, production of military goods overseas, also diminishes military spending as a job provider.

Now the truth is that military budget and military spending should never be determined by the number of jobs it will provide. Hitler, Tojo and Mussolini all promised jobs and full employment via military buildup.

The military budget and amount of military spending should be determined by the nation's real—and we stress the word real—national security needs. And military security is just one of many national priorities, not the only priority.

Yet each time the military budget, or a weapon system, such as the MX missile, B1 bomber or Star Wars System (SDI) comes before the Congress, the Secretary of Defense, military contractors and affected members of Congress and senators—all are certain to argue that we must spend the money or build the weapon, because it means jobs, jobs, jobs. We call it job blackmail. No other segment of the labor force is subjected to such brutal economic determinism. We're not given credit for being rational, intelligent, thinking and principled Americans.

Let it be said, here and now, that I've never met a worker making weapons to kill and overkill, who wouldn't rather be making implements of peace and prosperity.

Yes, it is easy to see that as the military spending curve has shot up to ever higher reaches, the number of skilled, semi-skilled and unskilled workers employed in military production has been decreasing, both in absolute and relative terms. And $300 billion military budgets have not given us anything approaching full employment. In fact, study after study shows that the military budget comes at the expense of jobs in the civilian sectors of the economy. With the exception of some highly specialized engineering professions, military spending, as a job creator, has long since reached the point of diminishing return.

Most of us in the trade unions, who have members working in military production, have a great many more members in civilian jobs. They, along with the underemployed and unemployed, are the ones carrying the burden of excessive military spending.

But the reality is that in an economy that features planned and chronic high unemployment, in many communities, military production may be the only game in town.

And, if that's all there is, then it's difficult to tell those military production workers that a particular weapon they're working on ought to be curtailed or scrapped. We have to look out for their livelihoods, too. And that's why economic conversion makes all the more sense. If the federal government is going to draft or lure workers and communities into military production in the name of providing for the national security, then when they are no longer needed or are deemed nonessential to that purpose, the government, indeed, society, owes the workers and communities alternative means to making a living with no loss in income or their dignity as free and prosperous citizens.

Economic conversion would provide that economic alternative, would preserve that dignity, freedom and prosperity.

Reductions in the military budget and military spending are bound to occur in the near future. The idea is already popular, even among traditional hawks in the Congress.

Prospects of strategic nuclear arms reductions can be expected to impact much more heavily, inasmuch as a broader range of weapons and delivery systems will be affected. The IAM, by the way, supported the INF agreement and we favor strategic nuclear arms reductions, too.

Those reductions mean a good many workers are going to lose their jobs. Their communities are going to become economic casualties too. The time to prepare for these contingencies is before—not after—they occur. Economic conversion provides that contingency planning and relief.

What Do We Convert To?

A list or catalog of socially useful civilian products could well begin with the nation's physical infrastructure. By all accounts, it needs to be rebuilt and refurbished. Airports, bridges, roads, streets, sewer systems, water systems and waterways, rivers and harbors, rapid rail and metro transit systems are all wanting. Plants, equipment and skills currently dedicated to military production could all be adapted and redeployed into producing the hardware and services necessary to upgrade and expand our civilian infrastructure.

Budgetary constraints are limiting our momentum in superconductivity, while Japan, France, Canada, West Germany and the United Kingdom have all made major commitments to superconductor research. For the legions of engineers and scientists now laced to military projects, conversion to superconductivity research projects is desirable and feasible. The Office of Technology Assessment has released a report which recommends a federal civilian agency and program to push the U.S. ahead in commercial applications for new superconductors.

We're behind in development of safe, renewable, alternative energy source development; we don't yet know how to clean up our toxic waste dumps; and we're behind in new structural materials development. Money and resources now being wasted for the Space Defense Initiative ought to be transferred into those programs of substance and need. Our civilian space program needs to be revived and relaunched. The list of potential conversion projects that would benefit society, rebuild our industrial and manufacturing base, and accelerate improvement of our international competitiveness is nearly endless.

Economic conversion is both practical and idealistic: practical because it provides job security for workers and their communities; idealistic, because it permits workers to support the noble causes of disarmament and peace, on their merits, without fear of sacrificing their bread and butter — without submitting to job blackmail.

READING

3

THE MILITARY ROLE IN A CHANGING WORLD

THE WORLD IS STILL A DANGEROUS PLACE

Harold Brown

Harold Brown is Co-chairman of "Monitoring Defense Reorganization", a joint project of the Foreign Policy Institute of the Johns Hopkins University and the U.S. Center for Strategic and International Studies. Former Defense Secretary James Schlesinger is the other Co-chairman.

Points to Consider:

1. Why does the author feel that more should be spent on defense?

2. How can the cost of military spending be reduced?

3. What does the author feel is more important than spending money efficiently for arms we need?

4. How might the Soviet Union continue to be a threat to the West?

Excerpted from written testimony by Harold Brown submitted before the House Committee on the Budget, February 21, 1989.

My own belief is that regional conflicts have no more seen their end than have business cycles or the alternation of political parties in power.

This remains a dangerous world, despite genuine indications of new opportunities for changing old adversarial relationships. My own belief is that regional conflicts have no more seen their end than have business cycles or the alternation of political parties in power. Moreover, my view is that the American people can well afford to spend more than the 6 percent or so of GNP (Gross National Product) that they now do on national defense. Thus, I start from the premise that in a budgetary process unconstrained by political realities, it would probably be prudent to resume real defense growth at the rate of perhaps 2 percent a year after inflation.

But the budgetary process is not unconstrained by political realities, including the history of the past eight (or even 12) years. It is also very much constrained by the apparent unwillingness of the American public to divert from the 86 percent or so of GNP that it now spends on consumption, an additional 5 percent to defense investment and an additional 1/2 percent or so to foreign assistance. How real that unwillingness is, and whether it could be overcome, we won't know so long as there is a continuation of the present lack of leadership in the Executive and Legislative Branches to persuade the American people that such a shift is in their long-term interest. Under these circumstances, it is realistic to expect that defense budgets over the next four or five years are likely to be flat, that is constant, after correcting for inflation.

Getting More from Defense Dollars

Let me turn now to the issue of getting more efficiency and effectiveness out of U.S. defense budgets. In the first place, stability and predictability of programs and budgets are very important. Their opposites certainly waste a great deal of money in defense programs. Rapid expansion in defense budgets (and even more rapid expansion of programs) during the first half of the 1980s, followed by significant cuts during the last four years, have made for considerable inefficiency. As to the future, it would be extremely damaging for the Defense Department to plan on a constant budget over the next four years after inflation and then be faced with cuts of several percent a year in real terms.

I believe strongly that implementing cost cutting administrative

The M1A1 Abrams main battle tank is the standard against which all others are measured. However, continued domestic production of the M1A1 is in doubt, because DoD plans to field a Block 3 tank beginning in 2002. The M1A1 is slated for licensed production by Egypt after 1992.

Source: Office of Technology Assessment

reforms in our defense etablishment probably would allow savings of ten percent, perhaps even 20 percent of procurement costs. That is a substantial amount, 10 or 20 billion dollars a year. Unfortunately, there is no way that this level of savings could be realized in a period of time less than 6 or 8 years, even if an all-out effort to change the system began now. It simply takes that long to change things, and there is a lot already in the pipeline or contracted for.

Even more important than efficiency in the procurement process is the existence (or not) of rationality and of a single strategy and set of priorities in deciding the force structure. Without a Secretary of Defense willing to set such a strategy and priorities, assisted in so doing both by a purple-suited (that is, not oriented toward a single service) Chairman of the Joint Chiefs and Joint Staff and a highly qualified staff in the office of the Secretary of Defense, far more will be wasted in procuring imbalanced and inappropriate forces than is wasted in the

> ## MUSN'T DROP OUR GUARD
>
> *Despite the reductions in active forces to which the President and the Congress are committed, the nation must be prepared to field enough power in crises to protect our vital interests. To have adequate capability to reconstitute our inadequate military strength in the 90s we must maintain:*
>
> - *An industrial base sufficient to provide weapons systems, munitions, repairs, and supporting materials for sustained major combat operations.*
> - *Adequate plans for mobilization in response to strategic warning.*
> - *Adequate intelligence systems to provide that warning.*
> - *Trained and well equipped reserves to provide regeneration forces.*
>
> *The foregoing will require vigorous leadership to withstand the traditional tendency of democracies to drop their guard in peacetime.*
>
> Adm. Ellmo Zumwalt, **Conservative Chronicle**, March 18, 1990

details of the procurement process.

Arms Control

Finally, let me say something about arms control and about possible changes in U.S.-Soviet relations. We should not expect any large savings from a START (Strategic Arms Reduction Treaty) agreement, even one that cuts the number of warheads by a nominal 50 percent (and an actual 30 percent) on each side. Reductions from more than 10,000 to less than 10,000 warheads on each side will not automatically make a safer world, whatever the symbolic value and political value of such an agreement. Continuing to have a secure retaliatory capability that will assure deterrence of nuclear attack will require some continued modernization of the U.S. strategic force structure, especially if we want to improve the stability of the strategic balance and increase the survivability of our forces. There may be some money saving choices to be made in the strategic force posture, but they are unlikely to be dictated by or to grow out of a START agreement.

Whether or not a START agreement is accompanied by new

limitations on strategic defenses and on the Strategic Defense Initiative (SDI), my own expectation is that SDI will and should stay at about its current level in real terms. That provides a savings of up to a few billion dollars a year over the next few years compared to what some administration budget projections have been predicting. But I doubt that it represents a savings from what any of the realists in the Defense Department had expected the SDI budget level to be. If and when we get to conventional arms reductions and redeployments, however, there are likely to be opportunities for much larger savings than from strategic arms agreements, since about 80 percent of the Defense Department's costs are for conventional forces.

There is good reason to believe that Mr. Gorbachev and his colleagues recognize the limits to the political advantage that military capability can provide in the nuclear age, and recognize also the very much greater dangers of falling ever further behind in economy and technology. This would greatly reduce Soviet standing and influences in the next century. Thus, they probably do want to reduce the size of their own conventional forces, in Europe and elsewhere, for a variety of reasons. They want to make other use of the resources thus released. They want to ease the political situation in Europe and encourage Western European help to the Soviet Union in technological, business, and financial terms. They want to loosen alliance ties between the U.S. and Western Europeans.

Whether, if they are successful in turning the Soviet Union around economically and technologically, they will become a more dangerous adversary or will have to have made such political changes in the process that a more normal relationship with the rest of the world would have become inevitable is impossible to predict. And I don't know whether Mr. Gorbachev will still be the Soviet leader in five year's time.

We should not do anything that makes the balance worse than it now is from our point of view. Thus I would press the Soviets for more detail on just what they intend to do unilaterally, and work very hard with our allies to come up with some proposals of our own for troop and equipment redeployments and reductions that will reduce the prospects of a successful conventional attack, whether a surprise attack or one after a mobilization buildup. If we succeed, over the next few years, in reaching agreements on such reductions, there could be substantial budgetary savings. I would certainly not, however, make budgetary reductions in anticipation of such success.

READING

4

THE MILITARY ROLE IN A CHANGING WORLD

MILITARY SPENDING LEVELS ARE NOT SUSTAINABLE

Robert S. McNamara

Robert McNamara served as Secretary of Defense during the 1960s in the Kennedy and Johnson Administrations.

Points to Consider:

1. How much does the U.S. currently spend on defense? How does this compare to the 1980s?

2. On what other factors is national security based?

3. Discuss how the Soviet Union and the U.S. could cooperate in bringing about a conversion from high defense spending.

4. What would the author have the U.S. Defense Budget cut down to?

5. How would this compare to other western nations?

Excerpted from testimony by Robert McNamara before the House Committee on the Budget, February 8, 1990.

I believe it would be possible to cut U.S. military expenditures approximately in half.

Neither the Soviet Union nor the United States has yet put forward a vision of the post-cold war world, a new political framework within which relations among nations of both East and West and North and South will be conducted in the years ahead.

For 40 years U.S. foreign policy and defense programs have been shaped largely by one major force: fear of and opposition to the spread of Soviet-sponsored communism. It will require a leap of the imagination for us to conceive of our national goals, to think of our role in a world that is not dominated by that struggle between East and West.

But because of the changes in Soviet policy which have been initiated by Gorbachev, we do indeed face the opportunity to shift the basis for formulation of our foreign policy and our defense programs from cold war thinking to a totally new vision of super power relations. By such a shift we should be able to enhance global stability, strengthen our own national security and at the same time produce significant long-term budgetary savings and the resources to support a very much needed restructuring of the U.S. economy.

Rethinking Defense Spending

It is time, therefore, to rethink our defense programs to assure a clear articulation between the military force structure and whatever threats to the security of this nation we may face in the post-cold war world. We have hardly begun to do that. The defense budget calls for the expenditure of approximately $300 billion in fiscal year 1990. In constant dollars, that is 3 percent higher than the average annual expenditure during the past 10 years, when military outlays were higher than in any other decade of the cold war; it is 30 percent higher than it was in 1981; it is only 6 percent less than at the height of the Vietnam War; and only 10 percent below the peak of the Korean war expenditures.

I see no justification for such outlays. And certainly no justification for their continuation.

Our security depends on more than military force. That has been true in the past. It is going to be increasingly true in the future. Our security is a function as well of economic strength and of social cohesion. And today our position in the world is

"Trade you a used MX for a Toyota franchise."

adversely affected by economic weakness and by unresolved and mounting social problems.

As a nation we have been on an enormous consumption binge. We have been living beyond our means. We have been selling our assets. We have been borrowing heavily both domestically and abroad to finance an unprecedented expansion of consumer spending.

The resultant rate of increase in our foreign and domestic debt is simply unsustainable. While enjoying this consumption binge, we have permitted severe social problems to develop, problems which will plague our society for many, many years to come: destructive rates of illiteracy, unacceptably high levels of unemployment among blacks and teenagers, and a rapidly growing underclass. For example, in this city, the capital of the richest country of the world, 51 percent of all births are illegitimate; we have high and rising rates of drug abuse and drug related crime; there is a failure to adequately address the problems of the poor and disadvantaged, and we have severe distortions and sectoral and regional growth patterns; and a very, very significant deterioration of our physical infrastructures.

SOVIET CONVERSION

We wish to draw the attention of the international community to yet another pressing problem—the problem of transition from an economy of armament to an economy of disarmament. Is conversion of military production a realistic idea? I have already had occasion to speak about this. We think that, indeed, it is realistic.

For its part, the Soviet Union is prepared. In the framework of our economic reform, we are ready to draw up and make public our internal plan of conversion; to draw up, as an experiment, conversion plans for two or three defense plants; to make public our experience in providing employment for specialists from the military industry and in using its equipment, buildings and structures in civilian production.

It is desirable that all States, in the first place major military powers, should submit to the United Nations their national conversion plans. It would also be useful to set up a group of scientists to undertake a thorough analysis of the problem of conversion as a whole and as applied to individual countries and regions and report to the Secretary-General of the United Nations, and, subsequently, to have this matter considered at a session of the General Assembly.

Mikhail Gorbachev, Speech to the United Nations, December 7, 1988

One of the greatest achievements of the American political and social system has been its ability to support political cohesiveness in a society as ethnically diverse as ours. This stability depends on preserving a reasonable degree of economic equality among the various social groups. Recent developments affecting minorities and the economically disadvantaged jeopardize the preservation of that equity.

So, in the face of these economic and social problems, I believe it would be folly to spend more than we need for defense. I think we are doing so. I believe that Gorbachev has presented us an opportunity to reduce the risk of military confrontation between East and West and thereby to lower the cost of maintaining our security.

The point that he returns to more than any other when

discussing foreign policy is his belief that modern military technologies—and here he is referring to technologies affecting both nuclear and conventional forces—modern military technologies have rendered war between the Super Powers as an unacceptable means of achieving political ends. This I think is one of the major factors leading to his proposals for basic changes in East/West political and military relations.

Bilateral Relations

Conflicts within nations, and conflicts between nations will not disappear. But how different that world would be if the super powers, the United States and Soviet Union agreed, on two points:

First, neither would seek to take advantage of such disputes to increase or extend their political or military power beyond their borders. And, consistent with that principle, neither the United States nor the Soviet Union would intervene unilaterally in regional disputes.

Second, their bilateral relations would be conducted according to rules of conduct which preclude the use of force or the threat of the use of force. Consistent with that approach, the United States and the Soviet Union would initiate sharp reductions in, and would ultimately terminate, military support of conflicts between Third World nations and conflicts between opposition parties within those nations.

Agreement by East and West to support such a program would not only represent adjustment to the reality of economic and political change in the Third World, but it would be consistent with moves to dampen down and ultimately terminate the cold war.

I believe it would be possible to cut U.S. military expenditures approximately in half in relation to GNP (Gross National Product), from 6 percent to 3 percent, or even slightly below 3 percent. That would make available in 1989 dollars and 1989 GNP, approximately $150 billion a year. That sum could be utilized to help alleviate the very, very pressing economic and social problems that I have referred to, problems in both our own and Third World societies.

Now, lest it be thought that a U.S. defense budget of 3 percent of GNP is a fantasy, we should not forget that today Japan's defense expenditures are a nominal 1 percent of GNP. In NATO (North Atlantic Treaty Organization) terms that might amount to something on the order of 1.6 percent. But it is far below 3 percent. Canada's expenditures are less than 3 percent. And the average today of all NATO nations, excluding the United States is on the order of 3 percent.

In the 21st century the relative power of the United States will be less. But no nation will have greater power. And in absolute terms we can be far stronger than today, far stronger economically, politically, psychologically and militarily. Substantial reductions in the Department of Defense budgets now lying before the Congress are totally consistent with that objective.

READING

5

THE MILITARY ROLE IN A CHANGING WORLD

DEFENSE SPENDING MUST BE MAINTAINED

C.A. McKinney

C. A. McKinney is a retired U.S. Marine and presently serves as legislative counsel on behalf of the Noncommissioned Officers Association of the U.S.A.

Points to Consider:

1. Why does the author believe that the U.S. must maintain a strong military force despite "glasnost"?

2. Discuss the use of "cannon fodder" vs. "smart troops".

3. How would the author suggest improvements in military compensation?

4. What other areas would need an increase in defense spending?

Excerpted from written testimony submitted by C.A. McKinney before the House Committee on the Budget, February 21, 1989.

It's absolutely ridiculous to even suggest that the United States can adequately defend itself and protect nations around the world with a total force of 2.4 million, less than it had in 1961.

In spite of "glasnost," the world around us has changed but little. The United States continues to be the leader of the free world. Many foreign nations rely on it to safeguard their economic interests and their national security. As a maritime nation, the United States must depend on outside sources to provide raw materials and other products for the development of its commercial interests as well as a mobile, flexible, and strong defense posture. The United States cannot sit back and ignore its position in world affairs. We, the people of the United States, cannot follow. Our role is to lead.

Our nation needs to maintain a strong Army, Navy, Marine Corps, Air Force, and Coast Guard manned by quality personnel whose numbers are determined not by fiscal constraint but by the missions assigned to the armed forces.

To sustain the current high-state of manpower readiness now enjoyed by the United States, military compensation must be adequate, comparable, and fair.

Sustainability also is dependent upon quality-of-life programs that subscribe to the good discipline and morale of personnel in all components (regular, reserve, national guard, and retired) of the armed forces. Smart people are always more important to an adequate defense than smart weapons.

Military Manpower

The Administration and Congress appear to be playing an old game of relying on "cannon fodder" (untrained manpower) to counter-balance any future national military emergency involving the United States or its Allies. Rather than have trained manpower (smart troops) at the ready, the Pentagon prefers to place most of its fiscal resources into producing, buying and maintaining hi-tech weapons systems that only the manufacturer's technicians have the knowledge and training to keep in operating condition.

Every war or conflict involving the United States in the past 70-plus years has proved for the most part that smart weapons do not win the important battles. Time after time it has been the foot soldier, the sailor, the marine, the airmen, and coast guardsman who win the battles in spite of the availability of

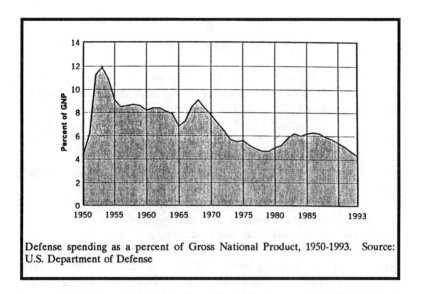

Defense spending as a percent of Gross National Product, 1950-1993. Source: U.S. Department of Defense

hi-tech systems that may not function under combat conditions.

Today, the missions assigned to the U.S. military services are nearly as great as they were in the 1950s and early 1960s. Yet, Congress endorsed a DOD (Department of Defense) proposal to slash military personnel strengths for FYs (fiscal year) 1988 and 1989 while increasing the missions of the services in FY 1989 to include drug interdiction.

It's absolutely ridiculous to even suggest that the United States, a leader of nations, can adequately defend itself and exert its influence on and protection for nations around the world with a total force of 2.4 million, less than it had in 1961. It's more ridiculous to insist that the United States can shift a large burden of its strategic and tactical missions to a reserve force that is 2 million less than its 1961 strength.

There's only one way to alter the future for our young people whom we may call upon to physically place their lives in jeopardy for their country and country-men. Make certain there are adequate numbers of trained personnel in the armed forces to assure a continued high-state of combat readiness.

Military Compensation

Active duty nondisabled enlisted servicemembers are not entitled to readjustment (severance or separation) pay although active duty commissioned officers are authorized such pay averaging nearly $29,000 for each separatee.

MORE VULNERABLE

What would the United States actually do if the country of Ugoria (we'll call it), whose ruling madman is seized one night by a commanding afflatus, gets up in the morning and dispatches a chemical or nuclear bomb aimed at Paris? Or, if we stretch intermediate nuclear capacity out by a few years, aimed at New York?

We'd see it coming in—there it is on the radar screen. Maybe we'd warn New Yorkers that they had 25 minutes to prepare against a Hiroshima bomb, or a killer-chemical bomb, giving New Yorkers an opportunity to do what?—except perhaps recall editorials skeptical of Star Wars, dating back to 1983. Sure, we could dump on Ugoria, which thereafter would be referred to in the history books as the "late republic of Ugoria." Effecting what? One less madman in charge of a subject country; big deal. Assuming that we proceed, pari passu *with the Soviet Union, cautiously to disarm to a point of rationality, we might find ourselves more vulnerable to 15 countries with a half-dozen launchers than we now are to the Soviet Union, with its 12,000 warheads.*

William F. Buckley, Jr., **Conservative Chronicle,** November 8, 1989

Active duty nondisabled enlisted servicemembers are the only full-time federal or quasi-federal "employees," including foreign hires, not entitled to readjustment, severance, or separation pay. This inequity applies to those enlisted servicemembers with as many as 19 years, 11 months, and 29 days of honorable service. They receive not one penny from the U.S. government to assist in transitioning to a civilian environment.

Military compensation continues to fall behind comparable private sector pay. Pay levels are below that which caused tens of thousands of military personnel to quit the armed services in the late 1970s.

We should increase basic military pay to more closely match that of comparable private sector pay and congressional intent.

We should also provide authority and funds to military services to pay bonus money to enlisted personnel forced to make early decisions concerning reenlistment.

Military health care has deteriorated over the years for many reasons, primarily due to soaring costs, inadequate personnel to man Military Training Facilities (MTFs), and the slow reaction by the military to modernize and equip its facilities with the latest in hi-tech health care systems and equipment.

We must provide adequate funds to the military to recruit, retain, and hire adequate numbers of health professionals and technicians and administrative personnel to man and to modernize and equip military treatment facilities.

We need to provide adequate funds for Morale, Welfare, and Recreational (MWR) facilities and programs necessary for the good order, discipline, and morale of military personnel, particularly single and junior enlisted servicemembers.

The Coast Guard Reserve is not receiving the budgetary support it deserves to carry out its assigned mission. Congress should authorize DOD to report on the feasibility of including guard and reserve personnel in the non-subsidized group health insurance program now available to former military personnel and certain dependents.

The absence of proper health care has an adverse effect on readiness, recruiting, and retention of guard and reserve personnel. Non-availability of affordable health insurance plus the possibility of catastrophic illness affects the servicemember's deployability. Lack of medical insurance coverage has resulted in general neglect of vital health care for these servicemembers and their families.

Reading & Reasoning

INTERPRETING EDITORIAL CARTOONS

This activity may be used as an individualized study guide for students in libraries and resource centers or as a discussion catalyst in small group and classroom discussions.

Although cartoons are usually humorous, the main intent of most political cartoonists is not to entertain. Cartoons express serious social comment about important issues. Using graphic and visual arts, the cartoonist expresses opinions and attitudes. By employing an entertaining and often light-hearted visual format, cartoonists may have as much or more impact on national and world issues as editorial and syndicated columnists.

Points to Consider

1. Examine the cartoon in this activity. (See next page)

2. How would you describe the message of this cartoon? Try to describe this message in one to three sentences.

3. Do you agree with the message expressed in the cartoon? Why or why not?

4. Does the cartoon support the author's point of view in any of the readings in this chapter? If the answer is yes, be specific about which reading or readings and why.

Fallout

CHAPTER 2

ECONOMIC CONVERSION: SWORDS INTO PLOWSHARES

6. ECONOMIC CONVERSION NEEDS GOVERNMENT DIRECTION   39

   Jonathan Feldman

7. GOVERNMENT PLANNING WILL NOT WORK   46

   William Poole

8. ECONOMIC CONVERSION WILL PROMOTE PEACE AND JUSTICE   52

   Amata Miller

9. ECONOMIC CONVERSION HAS BEEN A FAILURE   58

   U.S. Arms Control Annual Report

READING

6 ECONOMIC CONVERSION: SWORDS INTO PLOWSHARES

ECONOMIC CONVERSION NEEDS GOVERNMENT DIRECTION

Jonathan Feldman

Jonathan Feldman is current Program Director at the National Commission for Economic Conversion and Disarmament.

Points to Consider:

1. Summarize the concept of economic conversion in one or two sentences.

2. Explain how economic conversion would affect the budget deficit and employment in the U.S.

3. Why would local lawmakers be reluctant to support economic conversion in their city or state? Provide an example.

4. Who would provide the funding for economic conversion?

Excerpted from congressional testimony by Jonathan Feldman before the House Subcommittee on Economic Stabilization of the Committee on Banking, Finance and Urban Affairs, June 29, 1988.

Economic conversion planning is needed to counter fears that peace means depression, and to help repair decay in U.S. industry and infrastructure.

Economic conversion is the political, economic and technical process for assuring an orderly transformation of labor, machinery and other economic resources now being used for military-oriented purposes to alternative civilian uses. Economically, conversion requires planning for new markets, products and research and development for industrial facilities, laboratories, training institutions, military bases and other military contractors. Politically, conversion is a means for building constituencies for peace in America by providing economic options for those who derive their income and profits from military production. The formal institution of a conversion plan for military facilities requires a preplanning period in which managers and workers develop an inventory of workers' skills, and the capacities of factories and machines, and match them with the new requirements created by civilian products and markets.

Economic conversion planning is needed to counter fears that peace means depression, and to help repair decay in U.S. industry and infrastructure.

Options for Military Firms and Laboratories

The scope of civilian markets is increased by "alternative infrastructure planning," in which local communities and governments draw up an inventory of capital projects and social service needs. Investment in such projects would constitute major new markets for converted industries. Funding for these investments would depend on a national program of defense cutbacks and matching civilian expenditures to rebuild the domestic economy by retooling military firms, retraining defense workers and repairing critical facilities such as roads, bridges, rail lines and the nation's housing stock. Pat Choate, senior policy analyst, warns that "much of America's infrastructure is on the verge of collapse." He estimated in 1982 that local, state and federal governments would have to spend from 2.5 to 3 trillion dollars during the following decade (slightly more than all planned defense outlays in the same period) just to maintain today's level of service on public facilities.

But, targeted public investments in infrastructure (open to competitive bidding) can create opportunities and incentives for military contractors to move towards civilian production.

Investment in infrastructure would not be another liberal public works pork barrel. Rather, combined with new investments in civilian research and development, it would help restore the competitive base of the economy. Conversion linked to such investments would bring into creation new civilian facilities that were not solely absorbers of tax dollars (as military contractors often are) but generators of tax revenue.

An alternative to scientific and engineering resources devoted to the military can be found in the creation of a new national research agenda. It would require the expansion of research agendas, including, for example, renewable energy resources such as solar power, hydro-electricity, co-generation and alcohol fuels from biomass. Such energy research, together with investments in new production technologies and civilian applications of computers, would help restore the competitive edge to America's waning civilian economy. A new research

IKE'S WARNING

Eisenhower, in his farewell address as President on January 17, 1961, noted the emergence of a "permanent armaments industry of vast proportions" in the United States and acknowledged the "imperative need" of industry and government to manage it jointly.

Today, the military-industrial complex — in Eisenhower's enduring phrase — is larger and more pervasive than he could have imagined. Linked by profit and patriotism, the arms services, corporations, scientists, engineers, consultants and members of Congress form a loose confederation that reaches almost every corner of U.S. society.

Dean Kleckner, **Washington Post**, 1990.

---

agenda would provide the nation's military-dependent universities and laboratories with options as defense budget cuts threaten the Strategic Defense Initiative and other high technology research programs. Universities can also play an important role in retraining defense-dependent workers and engineers.

Conversion as an Economic Adjustment Mechanism

Conversion planning and practice has become increasingly important as a means of addressing the economic dislocation that comes from defense cutbacks carried out in response to arms control agreements and military budget reductions. The December 1987 summit bringing together President Reagan and Soviet General Secretary Gorbachev for the signing of the Intermediate Nuclear Forces agreement symbolized the growing commitment of political leaders in both nations to cut national defense spending as a way to cope with domestic economic problems. The 1986-87 discussions in the press about arms reductions have suggested that the U.S. and USSR might consider cuts as great as 50 percent of existing strategic nuclear arsenals.

On the American side, a primary motivation for such military reductions is the huge federal budget deficit. The scope of the conversion problem confronting the nation is suggested by the growth of the military budget under President Reagan. A report by the Center for Defense Information in 1987 found that "preparations for war have cost the United States $2 trillion since 1981."

42

The constraints imposed by the budget deficit are not the only rationale for conversion planning. The military budget represents a vast capital fund spent on non-productive weapons systems and personnel. These expenditures represent a growing economic problem because they divert resources from useful economic endeavors. By 1988, the combined effects of the military economy on the budget and the diversion of resources have helped transform the United States into a "second rate industrial economy."

Planning Time

The economic instability created by military budget cuts warrants the implementation of a comprehensive disarmament plan. Defense managers, workers and industries need to act in response to a readily identifiable timetable in which defense cuts can be predicted in advance. A two-year lead time is needed for industries to plan the full details of changing an industrial facility from military to civilian products. These activities include: market studies, selection of new product lines, refashioning of machinery and production layouts, investigation of new materials and arranging sources of supply. Planning for conversion for civilian production at the time of World War II began as early as 1943, or two years before the end of the War. In an April 28, 1943, letter to the War Production Board, David C. Prince, Vice-President of the General Electric Company stated that: "The very least time during which a new product can be conceived, models made and tested and pilot plant production initiated is of the order of two years."

Barriers to Conversion Planning

Unlike the World War II period, industries producing defense goods have become specialized and dedicated to military production. Powerful economic and political incentives have acted as barriers to civilian production in such firms. Defense workers and engineers have become accustomed to the work habits and design requirements of government-subsidized cost-plus contracts which reward waste rather than competitive efficiency. Marketing by such firms is not based on cultivating relationships with dispersed consumers, but on political connections and knowledge of complicated legal and administrative requirements designed to satisfy the requirements of the Pentagon bureaucracy.

Defense dependency has increased dramatically in a host of industries and their states. Such military dependency has raised economic and political barriers to civilian conversion in such industry. As a result, national conversion legislation must mandate pre-planning by workers and managers. In the past, top military managers have resisted planning for conversion to the point that they have sacrificed facilities to permanent closure rather than propose their reuse for civilian purposes through conversion.

If legislators felt secure that disarmament was linked to job-creation (or preservation) through conversion, then they would be more likely to vote down excessive arms spending and oppose foreign policies that require a huge military commitment.

The Pentagon has actively resisted reductions in military expenditure. In October of 1987 *The New York Times* reported that the Defense Department was . . . planning extensive layoffs of civilian employees and deep cuts in the work of small contractors in an effort to generate a political backlash against Congress for budget cuts, according to Pentagon officials.

These officials argued that "labor leaders and laid-off workers would register strong protests to their Congressmen and would exert considerable pressure in an election year to have the cuts reversed." A number of trade unions and the AFL-CIO's Industrial Union Department nonetheless have actively supported national conversion legislation as a way to bring economic security to their workers and assist peaceful planning in the economy. As defense cuts are seen as inevitable, political representatives and their labor and management constituents will be more willing to consider conversion planning.

Planning for Peace and Budget Reductions

Economic conversion planning and reversing the arms race (by mutual agreement) are interlinked. A nation with conversion plans in hand is able to enter disarmament negotiations without fear of causing domestic upheavals as millions of people must change their work. Disarmament steps become an economic opportunity and not a penalty in the presence of competent conversion plans. A fear of peace among many Americans is more than a grim jest. Such fear is rooted in the belief that there is no visible, serious alternative to the military economy as a direct source of jobs and income. That understanding is dispelled by confidence in conversion plans.

A comprehensive disarmament treaty, depending on mutual and verifiable arms reductions by the U.S., USSR and other nations, would further the scope of public investment, help reverse the arms race and allow for predictable conversion planning. Economic conversion planning becomes more and more crucial as disarmament is implemented with other nation states. The conversion of military products to alternative civilian uses provides workers with the assurance that disarmament needn't mean displacement. Military firms, their employees properly retrained and their machinery retooled for civilian work, could become independent of the subsidy controlled by the Pentagon. The nation's industrial production base would become linked instead to the rational allocation and organization of plant resources, competitive efficiency and planning by workers and managers to meet the demands of new markets.

If military firms convert to civilian production, the interests of workers, managers and their political representatives will gradually become more removed from military budgets and an orientation toward serving military objectives. The conversion of the military economy allows expanding expenditures on needed capital projects and vital social services. To take one example, converted military factories could produce such products as pre-fabricated houses to provide shelter for the homeless. Returning to the infrastructure problem, in New York State alone officials estimate that it would cost $2.5 billion to restore the 371 worst bridges to health.

Where are such funds to come from? The traditional answer to this question has ranged from proposals for new user fees on highways to an assortment of sales, corporate and income taxes. Certainly some taxes may be needed to confront the constraints on the national treasury created by multibillion dollar budget deficits. But much savings are to be found by reaching a comprehensive disarmament agreement with the Soviet Union with strict verification procedures and reciprocal arms reductions.

Conversion will allow for military budget reductions, and free up budgetary resources. It also provides an important first step in freeing up industrial resources for civilian production of bridges, housing and mass transit.

READING

7

ECONOMIC CONVERSION:
SWORDS INTO PLOWSHARES

GOVERNMENT PLANNING WILL NOT WORK

William Poole

William Poole is a Professor of Economics at Brown University.

Points to Consider:

1. Summarize the author's main argument against government planning for economic conversion.

2. Why should conversion rely on established economic policies?

3. Compare and contrast this viewpoint with that of the previous reading. How are they similar/different?

4. What specific problems are encountered when government assists with economic conversion?

Excerpted from congressional testimony by William Poole before the House Subcommittee on Procurement, Tourism, and Rural Development of the Committee on Small Business, May 18, 1990.

We will have no more success in using government to plan the conversion of our defense industries to the civilian economy than Soviet planners have had in managing the Soviet economy.

As a child of the 1930s, I have never known true peace. Hitler was rapidly growing stronger at the time I was born. We fought World War II. There were a few hopeful years after the war during which the United States demobilized its wartime defense establishment, but we soon learned that we had to live with the fear of another war that would be even more devastating if it were to come. We have suffered through the tensions of the Cold War for more than forty years.

In 1989 a peaceful revolution swept through Eastern Europe, and the Soviet Union continued on a path toward liberalization that it had begun several years before. Our nation had always understood the attractions of freedom. Those ideals, combined with the steadfastness of U.S. policy over many years, are responsible for this day. Some will say, "we won," but the truth of the matter is that the people of Eastern Europe and the Soviet Union are the biggest winners. Freedom won; we all won. Unfortunately the world is still, of course, a dangerous place in many respects, but it is much less dangerous than it was a year ago.

Now what? How do we beat swords into plowshares?

It is often easiest to understand our own problems by studying similar problems elsewhere. No evidence is more relevant than the failure of central economic planning in the Soviet bloc. We will have no more success in using government to plan the conversion of our defense industries to the civilian economy than Soviet planners have had in managing the Soviet economy. That is the place to begin this discussion—central planning doesn't work. Government in the United States will not be able to plan successful conversion of defense-based industries to non-defense products and services. These firms will have to find their own way.

Reliance on Established Federal Policies

Having made the basic point that central planning doesn't work, let me add that we should not underestimate the constructive role already being played by established features of federal policy. There is an array of automatic stabilizers built into the structure of fiscal policy. Unemployment benefits

provide a cushion for workers who become temporarily unemployed. Those who are close to retirement age can take early social security benefits if they choose to do so. The corporate tax system permits carry-forwards and carry-backs that provide some assistance to firms that are temporarily losing money. The United States has the best capital markets in the world; firms can readily raise capital to finance promising new ventures. We should not forget that our capital markets are effective in part because federal regulatory policies promote market efficiency and public confidence in the honesty of these markets. I do not welcome unemployment and adjustment pains, but know of no better way to manage the transition than to rely on the market.

Economic Policy

Overall economic policy is also extremely important. Adjustment to change is most difficult in a weak economy, when it is hard for newly unemployed workers to find new jobs and for firms to launch new products. The Federal Reserve did a marvelous job in the 1980s in bringing inflation down and then keeping the economy on a reasonably smooth growth path with moderate inflation. I believe that the Fed will continue to be

NO WELFARE CENTER

The Department of Defense is not a Federal welfare center for every town that is going to feel the economic pain of impending cuts in defense spending.

Congressman William L. Dickenson of Alabama in a speech before the U.S. House of Representatives, September 12, 1990.

---

successful in the future. A minor recession is always possible, but I am convinced that any recession will indeed be mild. Federal tax policy also had a lot to do with the economy's success in the 1980s. Tax reform increased incentives for work and investment. We should be extremely careful that the current budget debates do not lead to changes in the tax law that would reverse these gains.

There are at least four reasons for emphasizing the importance of established general policies. I'll discuss these reasons in turn.

First, established policies are much more pervasive and deeply-rooted than anything we might add to deal with defense industry conversion issues today. We want to be sure that established policies are sound, which I believe they generally are.

Second, conversion problems will affect many firms that cannot be reasonably defined to be defense-based. Defense industries buy many standard materials and parts from other firms. Defense cut-backs will affect a wide range of firms, and we should deal with all the effects and not just the most direct and obvious ones. It is the lack of understanding—indeed, the impossibility of complete understanding—of all the remote and indirect effects of policies that is at the heart of the failure of central planning. Markets are intimately connected one to another; intervening in one place has effects elsewhere.

Third, we should emphasize general policies and not policies targeted toward defense-based industries per se because the government should treat everyone in similar circumstances in the same way. Shouldn't a firm whose market is impacted by foreign trade, or by technological change in the civilian economy, or by changes in women's fashions, have just as much claim to federal assistance as defense-based firms? Unemployment is unemployment, and business losses are

49

business losses however they might arise.

Fourth, there is the problem of government budgets. All levels of government are hard-pressed today. Whomever we might blame for this situation, the plain fact of the matter is that the government will not be spending large sums on new programs. Reductions in defense expenditures provide an opportunity to reduce the federal budget deficit without severely cutting back on higher-priority programs or raising taxes substantially. There is no chance—repeat, no chance—of a substantial new federal program to help convert defense-based industries. I personally think this situation is fortunate, for I have no confidence that the federal government could sensibly spend substantial amounts in this area. But whatever one's view on the matter, substantial new spending is not in the cards. It would be a terrible mistake to lead defense-based firms and their employees to believe that substantial federal spending will be available to help in the transition. Such an expectation is bound to be disappointed; the longer the hope for federal help delays needed adjustment, the harder the ultimate adjustment will be. Firms and their employees should recognize that they are on their own, except for established government policies that apply to everyone.

Improving Established Policies

This is not the place for a dissertation on how to improve overall economic policy in the United States. I will touch upon three areas that seem especially relevant.

Sale of Federal Government Property. As defense spending shrinks, certain defense installations and bases will be shut down. In some cases, the property involved is well-located for industrial development. The federal government should sell these properties as soon as possible. Indeed, I urge the government to sell properties in advance of the time bases are shut down so that private development can begin as soon as the government pulls out. Our procedures for disposing of property the federal government no longer needs are cumbersome. This is a correctable problem, and I urge the Congress to correct it.

Liberalization of Export Controls. Firms are presently burdened with many constraints on exports of goods of potential military value abroad. I know that liberalization of export policy is now under way and urge that the liberalization be pushed. We can do our exporting firms a favor at the same time we help Eastern Europe countries to develop their economies. These economies need computers and other equipment; our firms need to sell computers and other equipment. Let's make a deal.

Capital Gains Tax Reform. The capital gains tax issue is a contentious one, but it is important in this context because we need to do everything we possibly can to provide incentives for the private economy to adjust to reductions in defense expenditures. Mobilizing private capital is one of the keys to success in this transition from defense production to civilian production.

I would not provide a special, lower tax rate for capital gains, because I believe that the general principle of treating all income the same is extremely important for maintaining the integrity of tax reform. My proposal is not to put capital gains in a tax-favored position, but to eliminate the possibility that capital gains can be in a disfavored tax position.

READING

8 ECONOMIC CONVERSION: SWORDS INTO PLOWSHARES

ECONOMIC CONVERSION WILL PROMOTE PEACE AND JUSTICE

Amata Miller

Dr. Amata Miller is an Economist and serves as Education Coordinator of NETWORK: The National Catholic Social Justice Lobby.

Points to Consider:

1. What theme is common throughout the five key values listed for economic conversion?

2. How could full employment be achieved?

3. What do the Catholic bishops believe the proper role of government to be?

4. How can economic conversion assistance help communities?

Excerpted from testimony by Amata Miller before the House Subcommittee on Economic Stabilization, June 27, 1990.

Five key values undergird the case for economic conversion assistance. These are religious values and they are also values which flow from the proper understanding of what the economy should be and do.

Assisting workers, businesses and local communities to make the transition from defense-dependency to civilian production is doing the right thing—morally, economically, and politically.

That assistance should be flexible, accessible, and generous enough to speed the transition process. Our nation cannot afford to waste time or precious resources, nor can we lay the burden of change on the backs of the people of defense-dependent communities.

The Economic System

The purpose of an economic system is to make the best possible use of the nation's scarce resources to meet the needs of the people.

The needs of the people are the reason for which the economy exists. To emphasize this the Catholic Bishops began their 1986 letter on the U.S. economy, titled *Economic Justice for All,* with the words: "Every perspective on economic life that is human, moral and Christian must be shaped by three questions: What does the economy do for people? What does it do to people? And how do people participate in it?"

As anyone who has taken Economics 101 will remember, the textbook assertion that the basic purpose of an economic system is to organize the use of a nation's scarce resources efficiently and effectively to serve people's needs—not to use people for private or social purposes and then discard them.

There are about 3.5 million civilian workers involved in defense production and close to 40,000 companies manufacturing for the Pentagon. These include some of the most highly skilled workers in the nation's most up-to-date manufacturing facilities.

To allow this workforce to be laid off, demoralized, and dispersed because of lack of planning and adequate assistance during the transition period would be a crime against them and the nation as a whole. To allow these facilities to stand idle or be sold off for private gain at a time when our nation suffers from so many unmet human needs and is losing ground in international markets would violate the basic canons of good

"Actually, I was hoping for a better return on the Peace Dividend."

stewardship as well as good economics and common sense.

Advance notification and assistance to foster alternative use planning prior to the termination of a contract or closure of a base is critical to the preservation of the local economy, the workforce and the facilities. High tech defense workers at Unisys in St. Paul, Minnesota, have identified 40 alternative products that could be made with their current skills and equipment. They are currently working to convince management that this is preferable to layoffs.

Each person has a right to employment and the nation has the obligation to help safeguard that right.

A Just Economy

This nation was founded on the principle that everyone has a right to the opportunity for life, liberty and the pursuit of happiness for himself and his family. In our economy that means the right to remunerative employment as the primary means to ensure these rights, since one's share of the product depends on one's income which comes (for the majority of

> ### WARDS OF THE PENTAGON
>
> *It's time to start planning the conversion of America's defense economy to civilian work. By conversion we mean political, economic and technical measures of assuring the orderly transformation of labor, machinery and other economic resources now being used for military purposes to alternative civilian uses. The political impetus for conversion is gaining momentum as a result of the relaxation of cold war tensions. Another stimulus to action is America's deteriorating competitive position in the world economy.*
>
> Seymour Melman, **The Nation,** April 16, 1990

people, at least) from having work in the marketplace.

The Catholic bishops stated clearly the ethical principles involved here: "Employment is a basic right, a right which protects the freedom of all to participate in the economic life of society." Full employment is an economic necessity; there is no economic reason why we do not have it—what is lacking is the political will to make it a reality.

Defense spending cuts have already led to layoffs of 29,000 workers, and there are estimates that as many as 1 million will lose their jobs as the military build-down continues. Adequately funding retraining programs tied to new jobs identified through alternative use planning can prevent this from becoming a human and national tragedy.

Study after study, as well as the experience of communities where bases have closed, demonstrate that economic conversion creates many more jobs than the military base or contracts did. What is needed is advance notification, locally participative alternative use planning, and flexible assistance from the federal government to realize the potential that exists.

Economic Planning

All groups affected by the transition should be involved in collaborative alternative use planning. No one group has a right to unilaterally make decisions which deprive others of their livelihood.

The revolutionary founding vision of this nation was one of

broad participation in the process of decision-making. Though the founders' vision of who should be included was limited by the culture of their time, the principle of mutual accountability was established. The Catholic bishops have expressed this reality in the form of a challenge to us today:

"The nation's founders took daring steps to create structures of participation, mutual accountability and widely distributed power to ensure the political rights and freedoms of all. We believe that similar steps are needed today to expand economic participation, broaden the sharing of economic power and make economic decisions more accountable to the common good."

One goal of economic conversion (as well as a means toward it) is collaborative planning and implementing of alternative uses of facilities and workforce. According to the principle of participation, all who are affected should be involved in the planning for the transition. This is necessary to build upon the experience and creativity of all parties, and to build support and positive energy for the process of change.

Management can no longer be allowed to act without accountability regarding decisions which cause severe economic disruption and hardship to workers and communities dependent on them. The Catholic bishops assert that it is "patently unjust" to allow them to do so. Broad participation in planning is also good economics.

As long time conversion activist, Mel Duncan, Executive Director of Minnesota's Jobs with Peace Campaign, puts it: "Conversion provides the opportunity to challenge corporations to consider social needs when making decisions and doing business, and most importantly, to discuss what kind of economy we want for our communities. Therein lies the hope for true democratic change."

Role of Government

The federal government has a responsibility to assist in converting these resources which it has used back to civilian use. The proper role of government is a controversial topic in some quarters. But the moral tradition is quite clear. As summarized by the Catholic bishops: "Government has a moral function: protecting human rights and securing basic justice for all members of the commonwealth. Society as a whole and in all its diversity is responsible for building up the common good. But it is government's role to guarantee the minimum conditions that make this rich social activity possible, namely, human rights and justice."

Or as Bernie McKenna, one of 900 soon to be laid-off military electronics workers in Connecticut put it, "If 900 people were left homeless by a natural disaster, a hurricane or flood, the government would have aid in there immediately. Well, we have a government-made disaster."

We must prevent any increase in the number of depressed areas in this country. We cannot allow a repetition of what happened in the steel producing regions in the 1980s. Corporations simply abandoned the areas, leaving a skilled workforce without alternatives. When the Youngstown coalition appealed to President Jimmy Carter for some assistance there was none available.

It is the role of government to help people, businesses and communities to help themselves in ways that will advance the common good.

The role of government in modern societies "is to work in partnership with the many other groups in society, helping them fulfill their tasks and responsibilities more effectively, not replacing or destroying them."

After a decade of anti-government sentiment, the nation is calling for "tough-minded compassion" says Isabel Sawhill of the Urban Institute—not a handout or relief effort, but assistance to people, business and communities to help themselves.

Economic conversion assistance is a true "supply-side" program with an assured payback from revitalized communities, businesses, and laborforce, not an after-the-fact mop-up effort.

As an example, when the closing of Kincheloe Air Force Base in Michigan's remote and economically depressed Upper Peninsula was announced in 1977, disaster was predicted for Chippewa County. But, the people saw it as an opportunity to convert the 4450 acre base to new, economically productive uses. Among other initiatives, the local private economic development corporation got a $4.3 million federal loan to set up an industrial park—it generated 1,000 jobs in 49 new firms. The county's employment base has increased by 10 percent per year over the past decade.

Economic conversion is another test of the moral fabric of this nation. We need economic conversion assistance legislation. It is the right thing to do, not only morally, but also economically and politically.

READING

9 ECONOMIC CONVERSION: SWORDS INTO PLOWSHARES

ECONOMIC CONVERSION HAS BEEN A FAILURE

U.S. Arms Control Annual Report

The following article was excerpted from the U.S. Arms Control and Disarmament Agency 1990 Annual Report. It is the Agency's 30th annual report issued under direction from the President of the United States.

Points to Consider:

1. Who is Seymour Melman and what did he do?

2. Why will efforts at "economic conversion" be likely to fail?

3. How is "economic conversion" defined?

4. How successful have foreign nations been that have had experience in economic conversion?

Excerpted from the U.S. Arms Control and Disarmament Agency, 1990 Annual Report, pp. 161-75.

58

Conversion efforts have rarely succeeded and none of the phasedowns in defense spending since World War II has required specific conversion legislation.

A leading proponent of conversion, Seymour Melman, observed in 1983 that:

* * * It is cause for very serious concern that, until now, no major military-serving enterprise has demonstrated the autonomous ability to carry out the sort of occupational switch that is needed to go civilian. Economic conversion is therefore an important policy idea that has yet to be proven in operation by American industry (Melman, 1983).

Professor Melman continues to be correct. As of 1990, there are very few concrete examples of actual conversion, in the basic sense of re-employing the same workforce and facilities to produce non-military instead of military goods. Most of the examples frequently cited are more appropriately called some form of diversification, usually involving acquisitions.

Existing Measures

Conversion efforts have rarely succeeded and none of the phasedowns in defense spending since World War II has required specific conversion legislation. However, the government has put in place a number of programs to ease any dislocations caused by such spending reductions in addition to the normal assistance all unemployed workers receive. These programs are also designed to lessen the economic impact on localities where defense industries are located.

Other Measures

Discussions with governmental experts, university study groups and industry representatives revealed that there were measures, other than the existing ones previously described, that were believed to be helpful in the on-going efforts of defense companies to conduct and implement diversification planning. Adoption of these measures, we were told, would further mitigate the need for any government-imposed conversion actions.

Participants in these discussions cited several reasons why conversion by defense companies was not appropriate at this time:

In today's economy, particularly with a relatively tight labor market, unemployment should not rise significantly, while growth

Reprinted by permission of **Star Tribune,** Minneapolis

in the commercial sector will adequately offset losses in the defense business.

Studies sponsored by some defense contractors have shown that if they were to attempt conversion projects, about 85 percent would be doomed to failure.

The defense industry should receive no special attention other than that which civilian industries and their workers receive.

Industry suggestions for ways the government could assist in a transition to lower defense spending were to provide incentives to promote a climate fostering innovation and growth in areas of importance to the United States. In particular, they felt that the government should:

- Make the transition to lower-level defense budgets gradual and orderly;
- Maintain R&D (Research and Development) funding at current levels;
- Reduce the budget deficit and thereby lower interest rates and encourage investment and long-term programs;
- Provide retraining and benefits for the displaced worker; and
- Remove impediments to exports of aerospace and defense

equipment.

- Industry leaders also called for multiyear defense budgets and appropriations to give them more advanced information on which to plan. Several argued that the government, particularly DOD (Department of Defense), should provide R&D money in advance of results, as it had before 1980.

Conversion Opponents

Opponents of conversion legislation assert:

Savings from a reduced defense budget are most likely to be small initially and increase slowly over time. Defense contracts would be cut back slowly or stretched out in such a way that the impact on defense workers would be minimal.

The largest defense contractors are already developing their own strategies for a transition, including diversification inside and outside the defense market and shrinking their companies. This transition is occurring without rises in overall U.S. unemployment levels. Many other major defense contractors already have substantial commercial business to cushion the impact of a decline in anticipated defense business. In 1985, major defense companies sold 53 percent of their products to the Pentagon. By 1989, that figure had fallen to 42 percent and continues to decline.

Some defense subcontractors in the lower category of technology may have already left the defense market over the last decade and thereby mitigated the effects of future defense shrinkage on the major contractors.

Local Economics

While the effects of defense cuts on communities will vary, local economies are becoming much more diversified than they were in the 1960s and are thereby making the adjustment to loss of defense contracts less severe now than it would have been.

Federal agencies operating under existing legislation, in cooperation with state and local governments, already provide technical assistance (e.g., planning grants, base or plant reuse plans, industrial development guidance, and market surveys) to help communities offset major defense industry cutbacks.

Studies have shown that successful local adjustment usually occurs because of the community's commitment to its future. This local commitment can then be supplemented with federal resources made available through state and local economic development resources.

The conversion of industrial facilities is exceedingly complex and requires skilled input to both the marketing and engineering aspects of the redevelopment process. Five years or more may be required from notification to start-up of the facility to produce and market a different product. Success may never be assured or achieved.

Detailed research has not identified a successful product in our economy today which was developed through a military-to-civilian conversion approach.

Foreign Experience

Studies of the European experience in industrial plant conversion have shown that the conversion produced only very limited success and was not cost-effective. On the basis of its extensive studies of nationwide and European experience in industrial plant conversion, Bettele Memorial Institute, an innovative R&D organization, found that the dynamics of the marketplace did not lend themselves to the conversion planning concept, particularly when the process was to be completed in a one-to-two-year time frame.

The experience of the Soviet Union is also worth considering. After President Gorbachev's speech to the United Nations on December 7, 1988, urging nations to undertake a policy of converting some of their defense production facilities to civilian production, a Soviet official noted that:

> It has been decided to set up a Central Scientific Research Institute of the Economy and Conversion of Military Production to formulate the optimum strategy for conversion and seek efficient forms of organization and solutions to the social problems that arise. . . .The adaptation of military production to civil industry mass production is a very complex problem. Conversion creates new seats of social tension. To eliminate them and enable people to obtain new training, 330 million rubles have been specially appropriated from the labor remuneration fund this year alone. As you can see, a wide, well-thought out program has been drawn up. So now not even skeptics can doubt that conversion is for real and for the long term (Smyslov).

Yet in spite of such optimism, the pledge of support, and the large pent-up demand in the Soviet Union for consumer goods, recent public comments from Soviet officials and academics indicate that several major problems exist with their conversion program. Various ministries that have been told to produce civilian products appear to be failing. They have no coordinated plan that would provide necessary political guidance and government supervision.

The Soviet defense industry is reluctant to transfer production capacity to civilian purposes since it continues to consider civilian production a secondary task. This industry also lacks the experience and the design and production infrastructure required to achieve quality output of the civilian goods it must now produce. Retooling some 400 defense plants without additional resources is proving difficult. Labor unrest has resulted from conversion-induced wage cuts as high as 30 percent for some working in the defense sector. In addition, the high technical level and production quality of defense plants have made the cost of civilian goods much higher than if they had been produced by civilian industry.

Reading and Reasoning

WHAT IS POLITICAL BIAS?

This activity may be used as an individualized study guide for students in libraries and resource centers or as a discussion catalyst in small group and classroom discussions.

Many readers are unaware that written material usually expresses an opinion or bias. The skill to read with insight and understanding requires the ability to detect different kinds of bias. *Political bias, race bias, sex bias, ethnocentric bias and religious bias* are five basic kinds of opinions expressed in editorials and literature that attempt to persuade. This activity will focus on political bias defined in the glossary below.

5 KINDS OF EDITORIAL OPINION OR BIAS

Sex Bias—the expression of dislike for and/or feeling of superiority over a person because of gender or sexual preference

Race Bias—the expression of dislike for and/or feeling of superiority over a racial group

Ethnocentric Bias—the expression of a belief that one's own group, race, religion, culture or nation is superior. Ethnocentric persons judge others by their own standards and values.

Political Bias—the expression of opinions and attitudes about government-related issues on the local, state, national or international level

Religious Bias—the expression of a religious belief or attitude

Guidelines

Read through the following statements and decide which ones represent political opinion or bias. Evaluate each statement by using the method indicated below.

- **Mark (P) for statements that reflect any political opinion or bias.**

- **Mark (F) for any factual statements.**

- **Mark (O) for statements of opinion that reflect other kinds of opinion or bias.**

- **Mark (N) for any statements that you are not sure about.**

———1. Taxpayers and defense workers have been betrayed by a corrupt Warfare State.

———2. In many communities, military production may be the only game in town.

———3. The military budget should never be determined by how many jobs it will provide.

———4. The American people can well afford to spend more than the current 6 percent of GNP on defense.

———5. We should not expect any large savings from a START agreement with the Soviets.

———6. $300 billion was appropriated for defense in 1990, three percent higher than the yearly average for the previous ten years.

———7. Current rates of military expenditures are simply unsustainable.

———8. Our security depends on more than just military force.

———9. Smart people are always more important to an adequate defense then smart weapons.

———10. Pay levels are below that which caused many military personnel to quit in the 1970s.

———11. It's ridiculous to ever suggest that the U.S. can defend itself with 2.4 million fewer troops than it had in 1961.

Additional Activities

1. Locate three examples of *political opinion* or *bias* in the readings from Chapter Two.

2. Make up one sentence statements that would be an example of each of the following: *sex bias, race bias,, ethnocentric bias, and religious bias.*

CHAPTER 3

MILITARY SPENDING AND SOCIAL NEEDS

10. MILITARISM DEPLETES THE   67
CIVILIAN ECONOMY
David Alexander

11. MILITARY SPENDING DOES NOT   74
HURT OUR ECONOMY
Richard Cheney

12. THE ARMS RACE HAS CRIPPLED   79
SOCIAL PROGRAMS
The Congressional Black Caucus

13. DOMESTIC SPENDING,   85
NOT DEFENSE, IS THE CULPRIT
M. Stanton Evans

READING

10 MILITARY SPENDING AND SOCIAL NEEDS

MILITARISM DEPLETES THE CIVILIAN ECONOMY

David Alexander

David Alexander is visiting Associate Professor of Economics at Wheaton College in Massachusetts. This reading was taken from a paper entitled "How Big Is the Military Economy: The Myth of GNP" which he began while he was a Lamont Fellow at Columbia University.

Points to Consider:

1. How is the Gross National Product (GNP) defined?

2. What percent of GNP is spent each year on military related measures?

3. How has the military-industrial complex undermined the civilian economy through resource diversion?

4. Briefly summarize the five resources that are diverted from the civilian sector by the military.

Excerpted from written testimony by David Alexander submitted before the House Subcommittee on Economic Stabilization, June 29, 1988.

We have mounting evidence that the civilian economy receives too little of several resources preempted by military production.

The debate over the harmful effects of the military on the civilian economy has taken on new force and urgency in the United States. In this debate supporters of the large military budget often fall back on a familiar first line of defense. The military budget, they insist, cannot significantly harm the economy because it comprises such a small portion of the Gross National Product (GNP), only some 5 to 7 percent of the entire GNP. Some proponents of the military budget use this percentage to judge the Reagan buildup modest compared with Eisenhower and Kennedy military budgets in excess of 10 percent of GNP. Others assert that the U.S. could readily spend a much larger percentage of its GNP on defense if necessary.

GNP as an Economic Yardstick

GNP measures the dollar value of all final goods and services produced in the nation in a particular period, usually a calendar year. It is well known that GNP is a very crude summary of the size of the economy.

Before looking at alternatives to the traditional use of GNP to measure the size of the military economy, we should emphasize that the figure of 5 to 7 percent of GNP considerably understates the amount of Federal monetary commitment to the military-industrial complex. This percentage typically compares the Department of Defense (DOD) budget to GNP. The DOD figure, however, leaves out several kinds of military expenditures and transfers: both foreign military assistance and the portion of foreign economic assistance which is defense related, the military portion of NASA (National Aeronautics and Space Administration) expenditures, veterans benefits, retirement pay for civilian and uniformed personnel, and interest payments on the portion of the national debt which financed previous military expenditures. After adding these outlays to DOD outlays, the military portion of GNP rises to between 7 and 10 percent.

Resource Diversion

When critics assert that the military-industrial complex damages the U.S. economy, they do not necessarily question the short-run creation of jobs and income growth attributable to the Pentagon.

. . . and the children shall inherit the debts of their fathers.

But we have mounting evidence that the civilian economy receives too little of several resources preempted by military production. The U.S. military economy diverts skilled labor resources from civilian industries to production of military weapons and equipment. It diverts several kinds of engineers and scientists from research and development (R&D) that improves civilian technology. Even before this it biases the direction of scientific and engineering sciences (and thus much education) toward very expensive, high performance military technology which civilian industry can ill afford.

The military economy, furthermore, has undermined the quality and cost-effectiveness of machine tools (manufacturing

> ## SPENDING STAR WARS CASH
>
> *For one trillion dollars you could—*
> *build a $75,000 house*
> *place it on $5,000 worth of land*
> *furnish it with $10,000 worth of furniture*
> *put a $10,000 car in the garage—*
> *and give all this to each and every family in Kansas, Missouri, Nebraska, Oklahoma, Colorado, and Iowa.*
>
> *Having done this, you would still have enough left to build a $10 million hospital and a $10 million library for each of 250 cities and towns throughout the six-state region. . . .*
>
> Dr. William Sloan Coffin, Jr., **Hunger Action Coalition Newsletter,** 1988

machines) produced in the U.S. By absorbing the taxes that Americans are willing to pay their governments, the military-industrial complex has also bled U.S. education, aid for the needy, civilian infrastructure and support for basic R&D. All of these diversions undermine the traditional productivity growth of civilian industries in the U.S. relative to foreign industries. Lower productivity growth in turn reduces our ability to sustain high civilian wages, to sell in domestic and world markets, and to expand employment opportunities for millions of Americans, notably such newer entrants to labor markets as women, minorities and the young.

Since a number of important resources are at stake for the depletion thesis, no single yardstick such as GNP indicates the size of all these depletions. We need distinct yardsticks to measure technical, scientific and skilled production labor, R&D funds and equipment, production equipment and infrastructure. Let us consider several of these:

- Diversion of Specific Production Resources—We can use rather fine categories of resources to examine the DOD diversion of resources.

Aside from specialized military industries such as tank production, in the midst of the Reagan buildup in 1985 the DOD purchased from 40 to 93 percent of the output of five industries; shipbuilding, aircraft and missile engines, radio and TV equipment, small arms, and aircraft and missile parts. The DOD purchased between 15 to 39 percent of the output of another 26 industries, including many industries which directly affect the productivity of other industries, from truck trailers, industrial trucks and turbines to machine cutting tools, iron forging and several primary metals industries to optical equipment and engineering equipment. While DOD expenditures helped prop up demand for many of these industries during hard times, if this output had been used by the civilian economy just for replacing old equipment, we would now have a more productive economy. *On these individual industrial measures, then, the military economy is from 2 to 12 times larger than the much cited GNP measure makes it:*

- Diversion of R&D Scientists and Engineers—The nation's pool of scientists and engineers has economic significance because they perform basic and applied research, develop new products and improve production processes. The DOD provides the most conservative estimate of the portion of scientists and engineers diverted to the military economy, 12 percent, or roughly double the percentage of GNP customarily attributed to the military-industrial complex. *It has been estimated the minimum proportion of scientists and engineers involved in military R&D at 30 percent,* or over four times the conventional GNP measure of the military economy. In some fields of science and engineering, of course, the proportion of engineers diverted to military production is much greater.

Between 1970 and 1984 the number of R&D scientists and engineers per 10,000 labor force population rose from 30.8 to 49.1 in West Germany and from 33.4 to 62.4 in Japan. Over the same period in the U.S., the increase was only from 64.1 to 65.1 R&D scientists and engineers for each 10,000 Americans in the workforce. Thus since 1970 West Germany has overcome more than half of the U.S. advantage in human R&D resources, while Japan has virtually eliminated the gap.

- Diversion of Research and Development Funds—Research and development of new technology is increasingly essential for commercially oriented enterprises if they are to sell in competitive markets and provide higher standards of living for their employees. R&D funds are spent on scientific and technical labor, instruments and materials. *The National Science Foundation estimates that approximately one third of all R&D expenditures in the U.S. between 1975 and 1985 went to the military, including space-related, effort.*

This raises serious questions about our ability to increase

productivity and to develop new products as rapidly as other nations, an outcome now confirmed almost daily.

- Diversion of Fixed Capital Investment – Fixed capital investment consists of one especially vital portion of GNP, the annual purchases of new and replacement equipment and buildings by businesses for producing goods and services. This investment channels many kinds of improved technology into the economy to increase productivity, and make possible higher wages and other advances in material life. Since productivity growth slowed down in the U.S. in the 1970s, analysts have often pointed to a decline in business' rate of replacing old equipment and buildings as a cause of the slowdown. While not all of this decline can be attributed to the military absorption of capital resources, *we do have considerable evidence of Pentagon preemption of fixed capital resources.*

DOD investment in durable goods (mostly military equipment, aircraft, ships and missiles) and structures amounted to 42 percent of the value of all civilian manufacturers' gross investment in equipment and structures from 1979 through 1984, ranging from about 33 percent during the Carter budget of 1979 to about 54 percent in 1983 and 1984 as the Reagan buildup picked up steam. On this measure the military economy is four times larger than the GNP measure makes it.

- Diversion of Public Capital Funds – A prosperous economy and a good material life require sufficient investment not only in producers' fixed capital but *also in the public infrastructure composed of highways and other public transportation systems, seaports, water and sewage systems, public buildings such as schools, parks and so on.* Military use of fixed capital resources thus also competes with these uses of physical capital and budget resources that could be used to renew and expand public infrastructure.

Estimating needs and resources available just for highways, bridges, other public transportation systems, water systems and sewage systems, the nation would need about $64 billion (in 1982 dollars) annually between 1983 and 2000 to maintain even low 1982 levels of repair and to meet growing population needs. We would fall short, however, by some $25 billion each year in tax revenues. This estimate does not count resources needed for educational and public health facilities, public housing, dams, parks, and so on. As we watch our infrastructure crumble, this is a particularly dramatic indication of economic depletion attributable to military capital investment.

While military outlays may stabilize the economy in the short run by propping up labor and profit incomes, they have inhibited the long term future development of the U.S. economy.

READING

11 MILITARY SPENDING AND SOCIAL NEEDS

Military Spending Does Not Hurt Our Economy

Richard Cheney

Richard Cheney was a Republican congressman from Colorado and has served as the Secretary of Defense in the Bush Administration.

Points to Consider:

1. How much has military spending been reduced?

2. Why is there still great instability in the world?

3. How is military spending related to the Gross National Product (GNP)?

4. How is this spending related to the total federal budget?

Excerpted from testimony by Secretary of Defense Richard Cheney before the Senate Committee on Appropriations, February 20, 1990.

74

The phenomenal growth in the Federal budget over the last 20 to 25 years clearly has been in other categories, outside of defense spending.

One of the things, of course, that people always are concerned about, and one of the arguments that I have heard repeatedly during my tenure as Secretary, and before that, even, was the extent to which defense spending is a burden on the U.S. economy.

The argument is often made these days that it has been an undue burden; and now that peace is at hand, we can, in fact, declare a dividend; and that this will allow us to spend less on defense.

The President's budget does, in fact, recommend spending less on defense.

Gross National Product

If you look at the chart on page 77, it is interesting, because it shows the percentage of gross national product (GNP) that has gone for defense over the last 45 years, going back to 1950. The peak on the left, of course, was the Korean war, with almost 12 percent of the GNP; for Vietnam, we spent over 9 percent; and at the height of the Reagan buildup in the early 1980s, it was 6.3 percent. If we follow the President's recommendation, we'll be down to 4 percent of GNP by 1995. That is the lowest level of defense spending as a percentage of GNP since before Pearl Harbor.

Defense as Percentage of Federal Budget

Another way to look at it is defense as a percentage of the total Federal budget.

Again, back in the early 1950s, or Korean years, it was 57 percent; 43 percent of the Federal budget went for defense during the Vietnam era; and 27 percent at the peak of the Reagan buildup. If we follow the President's recommendation, before any additional cuts imposed by Congress—if we follow the President's recommendation we will be down to 21 percent in 1995, the lowest level of defense spending as a percentage of the Federal budget since before Pearl Harbor.

The phenomenal growth in the Federal budget over the last 20 to 25 years clearly has been in other categories, outside of defense spending. We had a little bit of a surge in the 1980s and then started back down again.

Defense Cuts Since January 1989

- The 1990-FY Plan was reduced by $64.2 billion in the April 1989 Budget Revision.
- The 1990-FY 1994 Plan was reduced by an additional $167.0 billion in January 1990.
- The Defense Management Report contains reductions of $39 billion.
- Reductions to the FY 1991 Program amount of $22.4 billion since the Budget Agreement in April, including:

    program terminations,

    base closures,

    force structure cuts,

    deferrals,

    civilian hiring freeze, and

    military construction freeze.

This is just a quick summary of some of the decisions we have been involved in during the last 18 months wrestling with this. Again, if you add up the savings in the 1990 through 1994 plan, from the package I submitted last spring to what we have done subsequently in the package the President submitted this January, it is about $230 billion that we have taken out of this 5-year defense program.

Base Closures

Additionally, we have program terminations and base closures. We have some 20 programs that I have recommended terminating. In base closures, we have 86, approved by the Congress previously, that are now in the process of closing, and another 47 that are candidates for closure, including 12 overseas. There will be more base closing recommendations once we complete putting together the 1992-97 package.

Overall then, we have cut our military force structure in many significant ways.

We are recommending roughly a 2 percent per annum real decline in defense budget authority in fiscal year (FY) 1991 through 1995. This continues the trend of declining growth that began in fiscal year 1985. By 1995, the result will be a cumulative 10-year real decline of over 22 percent.

I think it is important to remind people that there is still a great potential for uncertainty and instability in the world; that

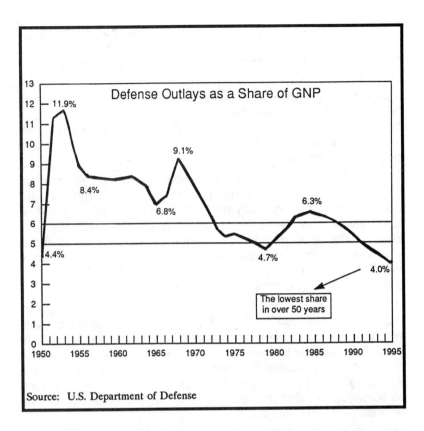

Source: U.S. Department of Defense

even with respect to developments in Eastern Europe, it may turn out that it was easier to tear down the old structures than it is to build new ones, and viable economies, and democratically elected governments in that part of the world. Certainly, the state of affairs inside the Soviet Union today is one of great uncertainty.

Whether or not we will see a successful transition to a market-oriented economy, the widespread acceptance of democratic principles and practices, and the establishment of democratic institutions inside the Soviet Union are still open questions that will only be resolved in the future.

In the meantime, as Defense Secretary, I have to worry about Soviet military capabilities, not just Soviet intentions. And Soviet military capabilities today are indeed formidable.

Future U.S. Military Capability

Given all of those assumptions, the U.S. still needs significant military capability.

First of all, we are going to have to maintain our strategic deterrent, because there is a growing proliferation of weapons of mass destruction and sophisticated weapons technology in the Third World.

Our strategic deterrent is something that we will continue to require for the foreseeable future, no matter what kinds of assumptions you make about international events. I think that deterrent ought to be based on both offensive capability and defensive capability.

Second, I think we are going to continue to want to maintain the system of alliances around the world and the forward deployed forces to go with them. I believe we can do that at lower levels than we do today. The fact is those alliances have been at the heart of our success for the last 40 years, and it would be a very serious mistake for us now, based on 6 months' good news, to abandon those alliances, abandon our ties with the world's other free nations.

Third, we are going to need to retain some reinforcement capability in the continental United States for those forces that we have forward deployed overseas. Whether you envision a scenario ultimately of having to go back into Europe, or perhaps deal with the problems in Southwest Asia or some place in the Pacific—Korea, for example—the fact of the matter is you want to retain some reinforcement capability in the United States on an Active and Reserve basis.

Fourth, we are clearly going to want to remain a naval power. We are the world's leading naval power today. There is no reason in the world why we should give that up. I think we can probably do it at somewhat lower levels. Maintaining the world's sea lines of communication has been and will continue to be crucial for us.

READING

12 MILITARY SPENDING AND SOCIAL NEEDS

THE ARMS RACE HAS CRIPPLED SOCIAL PROGRAMS

The Congressional Black Caucus

Points to Consider:

1. What major objections does the Congressional Black Caucus have against the budget of the Bush administration?

2. How does their alternative budget compare in revenue and spending dollars with the Bush budget? Give examples.

3. What provisions are made for children?

4. How is military spending dealt with?

Excerpted from the Executive Summary of the Congressional Black Caucus titled "Congressional Black Caucus Quality of Life Budget, FY 1991."

The centerpiece of this alternative budget is an un-yielding commitment to our most precious national resource—our children.

A nation's values and concern for social and economic justice are measured by the fiscal priorities established in its national budget. Judged by these criteria, both the Executive branch and a majority of the Congress failed the moral test of government in the decade of the 1980s. The ravages of Reaganomics, the extraordinary escalation of the arms race, and the mindless sequestration threats of Gramm-Rudman-Hollings, have wrought havoc on much of American society. Impacted are those most in need of help—the poor, the elderly, the young, the physically disadvantaged and the jobless. As a nation we cannot continue to condone this moral neglect and fiscal irresponsibility.

At the beginning of the decade, President Reagan challenged his critics to offer concrete alternatives, not simply to oppose his policies. The Congressional Black Caucus (CBC) took up that challenge and for ten years has offered comprehensive budgetary alternatives to those of the President and the respective Budget Committees. Through its budget document, the CBC has clearly demonstrated that the social and economic crises caused by the Reagan, and now Bush, policies are not a requirement of the budget process. We have demonstrated that humane and sensible alternatives do in fact exist, and that they can be found within the context of a set of fiscally sound and equitable policies.

The CBC has shown that we can provide for our national security, increase spending for crucial social programs, reduce budget deficits, and generate requisite revenues without increasing taxes for the vast majority of taxpayers. For FY 91 (fiscal year 1991), we have crafted a budget that seeks to capitalize on the dramatic changes occurring in our world. Changes in Southern Africa, Central America, Eastern Europe, and around the globe represent a dramatic opportunity to reprogram tens of billions of dollars that would be spent on armaments and to reinvest them in the human and physical resources of our nation.

The CBC FY 91 Quality of Life Budget offers an alternative vision for America. It addresses real human needs and potential by: (1) supporting proven social programs and creating new domestic initiatives; (2) providing for a national defense based not on obsolescent Cold War policies, but on evolving

international realities and constructive proposals for weapons and force reductions; and (3) making substantive progress in budget deficit reduction through true fiscal responsibility and equitable modification of the existing tax codes.

Commitment to Our Children

The centerpiece of this alternative budget is an unyielding commitment to our most precious national resource – our children. It emphasizes that commitment through increased funding for health care, especially pre-natal and pediatric; quality teaching and student assistance, from pre-school through professional school; better housing and job-training programs, especially in the inner cities; and a national determination to terminate the terror of the drug epidemic that is killing and maiming our youth.

The CBC is hopeful that the Bush Administration will stop continuing the policies of its predecessors. However, last year's budget indicated that Bush's "kinder and gentler" programs are as disastrous for the nation of those as President Reagan.

This year Bush's so-called two percent cut in military spending actually increases military spending by $7 billion for FY 91, while requiring substantial decreases in many domestic programs. For 1991, President Bush called for social program reductions of well over $20 billion. While President Bush calls for a few new

JOBS IN GERMANY

Studies in the Federal Republic of Germany have shown a need for 361,000 more workers in various social services. A small fraction of the expenditure spent on arms would be enough to fill these jobs.

In 1980, net costs per person undergoing vocational training in West Germany private business averaged 11,014 marks. Increased costs considered, every billion marks saved from arms spending could finance training for 60,000 to 70,000 young people. Since effective disarment measures would generally boost mass purchasing power, economic growth and employment, jobs could be guaranteed for all young people after completion of their vocational training.

Klaus Engelhardt, **People's Daily World,** April 2, 1987

---

policy initiatives, in virtually all cases, these initiatives are financed out of existing budgets.

These policies cannot be the policies of a great and just nation. They cannot be the foundation of a fiscally prudent nation, one that must allocate scarce resources among a variety of priorities. This is the year to begin to make constructive decisions and to reject the casual rhetoric of the national security bureaucrats and cold war warriors that we must proceed with caution. It is instead a time to redefine our national security strategy.

We must recognize that our nation will be ill prepared to enter the 21st century if our children cannot read, write and calculate mathematics, much less understand the high-tech world they are about to inherit. We must recognize that a nation that condemns its children to hopelessness and the lure of drug abuse is a nation that cannot remain economically competitive or morally strong. We must also recognize that our preoccupation with building better bombs has robbed our industrial base of vital research and development funds, of vital investment funds, all of which have dramatically reduced our ability to compete in the commercial world.

Any sensible definition of national security must include these and many other concerns, and must meet those concerns by the proper allocation of resources. This is the challenge that the

CBC has continued to meet and which we believe is addressed in this year's CBC Alternative Budget. What follows are highlights of our FY 91 alternative budget:

We hope that you will join with us in advancing a national fiscal program that can bring to an end the pain and misery of those who have been left so far behind in our society, and which can build upon the promises inherent in the most dramatic changes the world has seen since 1945.

The Alternative Budget

The CBC Quality of Life Budget differs from the Bush budgets, just as it did from the preceding Reagan budgets, in three principal ways.

First, it rejects the domestic program cuts proposed by President Bush and substantially increases social program spending, in particular for education, health, housing, employment, training, and for addressing the drug crisis.

Second, it reduces the military budget by some 7.8 percent in outlays, and 15.5 percent in budget authority for FY 91 principally through (1) nuclear weapons program reductions and (2) reducing active force levels, including initial troop withdrawals from Europe and Asia, as well as reductions in carrier-based task forces and troops stationed in the U.S.

Third, it raises new revenues by eliminating the unfair tax rate enjoyed by the very highest income individuals, requiring them to pay the same 33% rate currently paid by middle-income wage earners. It also imposes a surtax on the highest corporate taxpayers, those who received the largest tax reductions during the Reagan period.

In addition, the CBC Budget meets the Gramm-Rudman-Hollings deficit targets for each of the 3-year budget cycle years, FY 91, FY 92, and FY 93.

The CBC Budget spends $33.2 billion more than Bush for non-military spending for FY 91. It spends more than Bush for all non-military programs except for military-related space programs placed in the non-military budgets. It spends substantially more than Bush for education, housing, health, training, and food assistance, all of which represent the central focus of the CBC's reconstruction of America program.

The CBC Budget is $25.9 billion above the Office of Management and Budget (OMB) "current services" estimate of what it would cost in FY 91 to implement all non-military programs at their FY 90 level of service and coverage. Bush is

SURREAL BUDGET

As a compendium of the Bush administration's intentions, the surreal 1991 budget, which the President delivered to Congress, is an even more chilling document than might have been expected.

Bush's spending proposals carry few traces of his earlier enthusiasm for environmental protection, or of his Defense Secretary's rhetoric about massive military cuts down the road, or even of budget master Richard Darman's estimate on a Sunday talk show last month of an impending $50 billion peace dividend.

Instead, we got a record $1.2 trillion spending proposal featuring another bloated "defense" budget, coupled with further skimping on the country's urgent long- and short-term social needs and more tax relief for the rich.

Anna DeCormi, **Guardian**, February 14, 1990, p. 5.

approximately $10.8 billion below his own OMB "current services" baseline.

The CBC cuts FY 91 military spending (outlays) by $23.7 billion below Bush for FY 91.

The CBC raises $10.6 billion in revenues through tax equity measures. This in combination with a rejection of those portions of the Bush revenue scheme that we oppose on policy grounds (primarily the Bush capital gains proposal) would result in a net increase of revenues in comparison to the President's budget of $5.9 billion.

READING

13 MILITARY SPENDING AND SOCIAL NEEDS

DOMESTIC SPENDING, NOT DEFENSE, IS THE CULPRIT

M. Stanton Evans

M. Stanton Evans is a nationally syndicated conservative political columnist. He is a prominent conservative spokesperson and his articles frequently appear in the journal Human Events.

Points to Consider:

1. How does the author contend that defense spending is not the culprit of current economic woes?

2. What figures are used to further this viewpoint?

3. Why does the author criticize the idea of a "peace dividend"?

4. How did the "Great Society" affect the national budget?

M. Stanton Evans, "Domestic Spending, Not Defense, Is The Culprit," **Human Events**, February 17, 1990.

If defense consumes only one quarter of the budget, it cannot be the major culprit in the deficit melodrama.

Publication of the federal budget every year about this time is always the occasion for lots of partisan squabbling about the future tax and spending policies of the government.

This is an inescapable but not always helpful exercise, inasmuch as budget forecasts are largely guesswork. They depend on economic assumptions that may or may not be accurate, and are often miles from their intended targets. Over the past decade, official projections of what we were going to spend on this or that function of government have been wrong as often as not.

What the budget figures can tell us with some certainty, however, is what has already happened in the past, thereby providing at least some guideposts for the future. In this respect, the current document is especially useful, since it contains the final data for the Reagan years in Washington, providing an overview of budgetary changes engendered by the so-called "Reagan revolution".

Foremost among these asserted changes was Reagan's "massive defense build-up," presently the object of much derision. Among other effects, Reagan's emphasis on refurbishing the military allegedly robbed domestic programs of the dollars they needed, and was said to be chiefly responsible for the burgeoning federal deficit. These notions form the backdrop for current agitation about the "peace dividend" that can be harvested by slashing outlays for the Pentagon.

Scrutiny of the completed budget data for the Reagan era

Defense Spending as a Percent of Federal Spending	
	1983.....26.0
1961.....50.8	1984.....26.7
1964.....46.2	1985.....26.7
1969.....44.9	1986.....27.6
1974.....29.5	1987.....28.1
1977.....23.8	1988.....27.3
	1989.....26.6

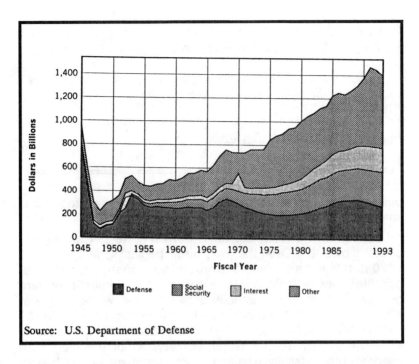

Source: U.S. Department of Defense

provides virtually no support for this widely held view of military spending. The accompanying table, excerpted from the budget document, shows the trend of Pentagon outlays as a percent of federal expenditures during the Reagan years, as well as under preceding administrations of the past three decades. (The pre-Reagan dates selected are those on which a new administration came to office.)

These figures are pretty self-explanatory. They show, for one thing, that defense spending under Reagan increased only marginally as a percent of the budget from the situation bequeathed by Jimmy Carter. In the Carter years, military outlays had declined to slightly less than one-quarter of all federal spending. Under Reagan, they got nudged up to slightly more than a quarter of all outlays—topping out at 28.1 percent in 1987, and winding up at 26.6 percent in '89.

This was indeed an increase, but hardly the massive shift in national priorities suggested by the usual commentary on the subject. In both cases, non-defense spending consumed approximately three-quarters of the budget, with defense absorbing the remainder. (Reagan, it should be added, had proposed much larger defense increases, but these did not materialize.) In view of the publicity accorded the Reagan

DOMESTIC SPENDING GREW

There was only one year of budget cutting, 1981, followed by seven years of rapid growth, growth that has accelerated in the 1990s.

John Cogan, **Wall Street Journal**, September 6, 1990.

build-up, what is most striking is how little these proportions changed from one administration to the next.

Looking at the historical data, however, we get an entirely different picture. Over the long term, beginning in the middle 1960s, there has been a tremendous change in budget priorities—away from defense and toward domestic welfare outlays. When John Kennedy arrived at the White House in 1961, we were spending over half the budget on defense, vs. 30 percent for "human resource" (i.e., domestic welfare) programs. With the advent of the Great Society, all of this began to change—progressively whittling down the share of the budget going to defense.

By the mid-70s, the Pentagon had been reduced to a quarter of federal spending, while domestic welfare outlays consumed one-half of all the dollars being disbursed by Uncle Sam. The Reagan years did nothing to alter this fundamental alignment, managing only to eke out a couple of percentage points of added spending for the Pentagon. At its peak, the "Reagan build up" allocated a smaller share of federal outlays to the military than was the case when Gerald Ford ascended to the presidency.

Moreover, even this marginal shift has been reversed in recent years. The share of the budget going to defense fell in both 1988 and 1989, and is estimated at 24.8 percent for this year. The forecasts of the Bush Administration have this dropping to 21.6 percent by 1995—even before "peace dividend" enthusiasts have worked their will in Congress. The latter number, if anywhere near correct, would be lower than the lowest low point of the Carter era.

From all of which a number of conclusions follow: One is that the Great Society obviously marked a basic watershed in federal budget-making, tilting our priorities away from defense and toward domestic welfarism. Despite all the hoopla, Reagan was unable to reverse this. Another is that, if defense consumes only one-quarter of the budget, it cannot be the major culprit in the deficit melodrama. That role must go instead to the enormous and permanent increases we have experienced in domestic spending.

It further follows that politicians touting a "peace dividend" are peddling a phony commodity. Far from a monstrous defense establishment crowding out domestic programs and pushing federal outlays out of control, the long-term data reveal a situation that is exactly the opposite of this. Renewed attempts to transfer dollars to domestic welfare programs, whatever their supposed merits otherwise, will intensify the very budget trends that have pushed us toward insolvency.

Reading and Reasoning

EXAMINING COUNTERPOINTS

This activity may be used as an individualized study guide for students in libraries and resource centers or as a discussion catalyst in small group and classroom discussions.

The Point

Economic conversion from the "Warfare State" is essential to promote peace and justice. Full employment is an economic necessity. Study after study demonstrates that economic conversion creates more jobs than the military base or contracts did. We must cut defense spending and convert to a civilian economy.

The Counterpoint

Economic conversion is simply another scheme to bleed the defense budget by billions of dollars and give it to social welfare "give-away" programs. Defense cuts will lead to massive lay-offs and severe economic dislocation. This should be avoided with an increase in defense spending.

Guidelines for Discussion

Issues are usually complex, but often problems become oversimplified in political debates and discussion. Usually a polarized version of social conflict does not adequately represent the diversity of views that surround social conflicts.

1. How do you define economic conversion?

2. What is meant by the term "Warfare State"?

3. Examine the counterpoints above. Then write down possible interpretations of this issue other than the two arguments stated in the counterpoints above.

CHAPTER 4

GLOBAL MILITARISM

14. NON-VIOLENCE IS THE WAY   93
    TO PEACE

   The War Resisters League

15. VIOLENCE CAN BE A NECESSARY   100
    EVIL

   John Garvey

16. STOPPING THE WAR AGAINST   105
    THE THIRD WORLD

   Michael T. Klare

17. PREPARING TO WIN LOW-INTENSITY   112
    CONFLICTS

   David Silverstein

18. A NEW MILITARY BUDGET FOR   120
    A NEW WORLD

   The Center for Defense Information

19. THE HIGH COST OF ARMS   127
    REDUCTION

   Malcolm Wallup

20. IMPOVERISHED BY RUNAWAY ARMS RACE 132
Christian Social Action

21. THIS IS NO TIME TO BEAT OUR SWORDS INTO PLOWSHARES 136
Thomas Sowell

22. EXPOSING THE ROOTS OF MILITARISM 140
Roger Powers

23. LIVING IN A DANGEROUS WORLD 146
A. M. Gray

READING

14 GLOBAL MILITARISM

NON-VIOLENCE IS THE WAY TO PEACE

The War Resisters League

The War Resisters League in the U.S. is part of War Resisters International, a worldwide network of concerned citizens who advocate social justice, non-violence and war resistance.

Points to Consider:

1. Why does the author believe disarmament to be so crucial?

2. Describe the Cold War "Bloc System". How will its elimination enhance international justice?

3. How can shifting social priorities contribute to conversion?

4. How could support of human rights direct us away from the "warfare state"?

Excerpted from an article published by the War Resisters League entitled "A Platform for Disarmament," June 1989.

93

Governments around the world bent on pursuing military power have neglected social needs to the extent that now one person in five lives in poverty.

For the past forty years, the world's governments have waged numerous "conventional" wars while building nuclear arsenals capable of universal annihilation. Peace movements around the globe have generally responded by campaigning for the elimination of specific non-conventional weapons systems or classes of weapons. Often, discussion of how to achieve real peace is put off to later.

The War Resisters League (WRL) believes a clear statement of our goals is useful in creating a context for our day-to-day actions. In this vein, we present a platform for disarmament—a framework for the movement toward a safe and disarmed planet. This platform was written by activists in the United States. While we cannot prescribe for others, we believe there is much general validity for these principles.

Disarmament and the Elimination of War

War is a social institution which must be abolished. Whether it is called Manifest Destiny, Holy Jihad, the recovery of lost borders, or revolutionary armed struggle, all war is a crime against humanity and cannot be justified.

We demand general and complete disarmament. While a nuclear arms control agreement or the cancellation of a new strategic weapons system may seem like progress, it only represents a momentary slowing of the rush toward destruction, and not a change in the direction.

New nuclear arms continue to be developed, and existing ones are still pointed at people in many continents.

Although conventional weapons and local wars do the great majority of the damage, nuclear weapons pose the ever-present threat of global annihilation. While working for general and complete disarmament, we single out the nuclear threat for immediate attention, and advocate a process of unilateral disarmament as the most realistic, attainable, and humane path to general disarmament.

By starting to reduce national reliance on the military, without excuses or conditions based on the actions of other powers, unilateral action can break the escalating cycle of the arms race. One step toward this goal of total disarmament is the elimination of nuclear weapons by the year 2000.

Reprinted with permission of the **Star Tribune**, Minneapolis

Local conflicts must be resolved with non-military approaches, respectful of the rights of the people directly involved. Only by dealing with the causes of conflict — political, economic, racial, religious, cultural, and territorial — can we avert the effects: death, devastation, starvation, and perhaps species suicide.

Nuclear energy use must also be eliminated. "Civilian" nuclear reactors and fuel processing facilities can be used to secretly make nuclear weapons.

By shutting down the entire nuclear fuel cycle, including uranium mining, it will be far easier to verify that no nuclear weapons are being made. Thousands of cancer deaths will also be prevented, the trend toward institutional and corporate concentration of power and wealth will be slowed, and land stolen from indigenous people can be returned to them.

Another important disarmament step is the elimination of the international arms trade. Buying, selling and trading weapons fuels conflict, while providing profits and political advantage for the few. The U.S. must get out of the arms business and encourage other nations to do the same.

U.S. supplied weaponry and military training is particularly damaging in the Middle East, which receives the lion's share of

NON-VIOLENCE WORKS

Non-violent protest didn't work in China.

So holds conventional assessment. Good try, brave students. You and your dreams of freedom thrilled the world for a few weeks. But the dictators and their guns won, and now bullets are being pumped into the skulls of dissidents rounded up for a second massacre. If evaluated by the measurement of body counts, China's student protesters were defeated smashingly.

The protesters were aware of both the other side's military power and its record of ruthlessly using it when provoked. **They knew another reality, too:** *Chances for achieving justice through violent force are far less than through non-violent force. Had Gandhi used tanks and guns, the British might still be in India, as they are in Northern Ireland today, which has no Gandhi.*

When the Polish government outlawed Solidarity and declared martial law in 1981, few foresaw the democratic reforms won by Lech Walesa.

Colman McCarthy, **The Washington Post,** July 1, 1989

U.S. military aid, exacerbating tension in a crisis-riddled region. All superpower involvement in the Middle East, including military support, arms sales, troop training, and troop deployments must be ended, so that solutions can be approached with international conferences of all involved parties.

Finally, we urge a shift to non-violent, civilian-based defense. No power on earth can control or govern the United States without the consent of its people. National defense policy should be shifted to encourage independent thinking and structures that would allow the American people to successfully resist any attempt at domination without the use of arms.

International Justice and the Elimination of the Cold War Bloc System

The root of military conflict lies in injustice. Especially in the Third World, harsh and exploitative regimes have often been propped up by the U.S. or USSR, in pursuit of national or business interests. Although the era of European empires has passed, new forms of domination and neo-colonialism continue to prevent national self-determination of many poor or small countries.

We also oppose the growing use of subtler forms of intervention—from the covert actions of the CIA, and others to strategies like "low-intensity conflict," where the U.S. funds militaries at war against their own people in places like El Salvador and the Philippines, or trains and arms opponents of regimes it seeks to overthrow, as in Afghanistan or Kampuchea. We reject the racism implicit in the Monroe Doctrine and other claims to spheres of influence, and advocate diplomacy based on equality.

The growing trend toward privatization of foreign policy is abhorrent. Whether through Contragate-style guns-for-hostage deals or by mercenaries or proxy armies, intervention is intolerable even if government would disclaim responsibility. Foreign policy must be openly conducted, democratically chosen, and respectful of human rights.

As part of moving away from interventionism, foreign military bases and naval ports must be eliminated.

Nuclear navies are particularly dangerous because they risk accidental or deliberate confrontations leading to global nuclear war. We call on all non-nuclear nations to follow Vanuatu, Aotearoa (New Zealand) and other nations' examples by outlawing port calls by nuclear capable vessels.

We call for demilitarized zones in Europe and an end to the bloc system which divides Europe into areas controlled by "us" and "them".

The present "peace" based on mutual threat must be replaced by consent to international mediation. Bilateral military agreements, which encourage militarism, facilitate intervention, and cause conflict to spread, should also be dissolved.

The United Nations and World Court must be strengthened and international law must be respected by all nations. National governments have to relinquish some of their autonomy to international authority if we are serious about settling conflicts peacefully.

In addition to supporting peace rather than exploiting wars, the U.S., and other industrialized nations must join international efforts to economically aid developing countries. The real enemies of humanity are hunger, disease and illiteracy. We are encouraged by the model of constructive economic aid set by Oxfam, and by Sweden, Norway, and Holland, which encourages self-sufficiency, independence, and technology appropriate to the local situation.

Shifting Social Priorities from Death to Life

Federal budget priorities must be shifted from the Pentagon to domestic programs. Governments around the world bent on pursuing military power have neglected social needs to the extent that now one person in five lives in poverty.

In the U.S., 60 percent of the federal income tax dollar goes to the military, and less than 2 percent to education. As the rich get richer, the poor, who are disproportionately people of color, are being deprived of their homes and jobs. Poverty and drug-related crime ravage the African-American community more than any other, and labor unions and other people's organizations are under attack.

People in the United States and all over the world are dying from hunger, homelessness, drugs, and environmental destruction. Instead of pouring our limited resources into more efficient ways of killing, we demand that priority be given to improving the quality of life by funding health care, housing, education, and other human needs. All the weapons imaginable provide no security if we are destroying ourselves from within.

We urge a more ecological and sustainable use of the earth's environment. One of the most important purposes of arms and militarism is to gain and protect the access of the privileged to limited resources. We believe that unjust distribution of the earth's resources leads not only to social evils such as poverty, but to their profligate and unsustainable use. This leads to such international ecological degradations as acid rain, destruction of rain forests, build-up of carbon dioxide in the atmosphere, depletion of the ozone layer, toxins in water and food, and the release of nuclear radiation. Recent floods and famines have probably been caused or exacerbated by abuses of the earth.

We must also address the cultural and political roots of militarism.

Domestic violence and violence against women is widespread at all economic levels, and children are taught that competition and winning are the most important values. Guns are nearly as commonplace as the TV sets which demonstrate their use dozens of times every evening.

Therefore, we must begin to establish a "peace culture" and start the demilitarization of our society at the cultural level as well as at the missile plants. From Rambo dolls to Junior ROTC, from violence on television to video war games, we must end the "military mania" brainwashing of our society.

Supporting Human Rights and Resistance to Militarism Around the World

We support the Universal Declaration of Human Rights, which spells out certain fundamental rights guaranteed to every person. These include the right to decent housing and employment, and the freedoms of expression, religion, and ethnic equality. The right to conscientious objection must be included with those basic rights; this right is crucial in dismantling the war machine.

We also support individual resisters as they refuse to cooperate with the war machine. This includes war tax resistance, refusing to register for the draft, and support for activists involved in nonviolent direct action and civil disobedience. We support all people at whatever level they are able to participate in resisting the military.

READING

15 GLOBAL MILITARISM

VIOLENCE CAN BE A NECESSARY EVIL

John Garvey

John Garvey Is a regular contributing columnist for Commonweal *magazine*

Points to Consider:

1. Does the author feel non-violence offers a solution to evil?

2. What dilemmas are faced by those who believe in non-violence?

3. How is the "Good Samaritan" story an example of one of these stories?

4. How is evil defined?

John Garvey, "Murderous Evil," **Commonweal,** September 20, 1985.

There are occasions when there may be no alternative to killing another human being.

In his July 12 Commonweal article, "Appointment with Hitler," Peter Steinfels raises some difficult and necessary questions. The question of our response to Hitler is of supreme importance, and it has not been dealt with well by those of us who believe that Christianity demands nonviolence. Steinfels rightly points out that such statements as "War never solves anything" or the assertion that all wars are fought ultimately for reasons which are exploitative, racist, based on misunderstanding, or simple devices to benefit the military-industrial complex—all of these duck the question posed by Hitler: What are we to do when confronted by murderous evil? The fact that the Allies themselves were guilty of evil actions and that all motives were not pure does not change this central truth: Nazism was uniquely evil.

Non-Violence and Morality

Pacifists have argued that to respond to violence with violence makes us no better than those violent people we oppose. That looks neat on paper, but in fact what does it mean? I may choose to accept violence against myself rather than be violent—I mean this in theory, because I am not at all sure that confronted with such a choice I would be able to accept what I believe I should do—but would it be right for me to accept the violence done to another person? If someone mugs me and I hand over my wallet and allow him to slug me rather than resist him violently, that's one thing. I am hardly working from the same place, morally, if I allow him to rob and slug an old lady while I stand by. Abstract nonviolence could argue equally for both courses of action (or inaction), but real morality can't.

Christians who believe in non-violence face a number of dilemmas. I believe that we must hold on to the belief in non-violence, and confront the dilemmas honestly without reducing them for rhetorical purposes.

Here is one dilemma: we believe that all human beings—not just those within our borders—are equally loved by God, made in God's image, and are, for that reason, to be revered. To kill anyone for reasons of state, or to allow any government to define other human beings as those we may kill (and this is something which happens in every war), would violate something central to our faith.

At the same time, it is right to ask what the Good Samaritan

Photo credit: U.S. Department of Defense

The Avibras Artillery Saturation Rocket Bombardment System Astros II multiple rocket launcher deployed by the Royal Saudi Army during the Persian Gulf War. The unit can fire rockets from 9 to 70 km with high explosive and cluster munitions. It is known to be in service in Brazil, Libya, Iraq, and Saudi Arabia.

would have done if he had arrived on the scene a little earlier. Would he have stayed in the background while the robbers beat the stuffing out of the victim the Samaritan later tended? The victim would in that case have been a victim as much of the Samaritan's nonintervention as he was of the robbers' violence.

One answer to this is that resistance does not always have to mean murder. One can resist, even forcefully, without killing. But what if this isn't always the case? If a Japanese pacifist were, by some odd chance, seated at the controls of an anti-aircraft weapon; and if he spotted the Enola Gay; and if, knowing somehow that it was about to drop the bomb, he refrained from shooting it down on the reasonable grounds that doing so might kill someone, would he have done the right thing?

What I want to suggest is that the way we have done moral theology is often perverse, and it is further complicated these days by the desire of religious people to make secular sense. The perversity is this: we have tried to find ways through moral dilemmas which ignore the mystery of evil by saying, more or

NATIONAL SECURITY

Defense is another area, along with economic opportunity and growth, where the Democratic Party has left its traditional foundations over the past couple of decades. The party of Roosevelt, Truman, and Kennedy understood that one of the most critical responsibilities of our national government is to protect our national security. These presidents all understood that the world is imperfect, and that although civilization has progressed in many ways, we still are imperfect enough to want to cause harm to one another. Unless you have strength, and show that you are willing to use that strength in international relations, people and governments will take advantage of you and you will suffer for your timidity. The United States should not go looking for fights, but we have to be ready to defend our interests and defend them widely and courageously.

Robert Lieberman, **Policy Review,** Summer, 1990, p. 27.

less, that any necessity becomes good by virtue of the fact of necessity itself.

If in order to save my family I must kill the madman with an ax because, given the situation I find myself in, there is no other real choice available, then I should not feel defiled.

The Reality of Evil

Human beings can find themselves implicated in evil despite all of their best choices; they can find themselves confronted at times with only two paths, each of which leads to an evil end.

Jesus referred to "the Prince of this world." There is something present in the world, in the life of each of us, which does not love humanity and which distracts us from what has been revealed as our salvation. It is a vanishing, or at least a diminishing, of this understanding which allows us to think of a Hitler as sick, rather than evil.

The reality of evil means that a person—free, and at the same time perhaps blighted by sickness—can turn to the desire for power and manipulation rather than to compassion and, because this exposes us to the will of others, to weakness; in this turning, a choice is made which allows murder to be born. Something which affects us personally allows us to make this choice, and it is not wrong to call it satanic.

What about the dilemma facing the person who believes absolutely in the need for non-violence, but who is confronted with occasions in which the only possible moral action seems to demand a violence which will lead to the evil of another's death? It may be that there are times when the only thing to do is accept violence and then repent.

This makes sense to me, as does the possibility that someone might have to shed blood. On the one hand, it is important to bear witness to the fact that the life of any human being, even a bloodthirsty one, is sacred. On the other, there are occasions when there may be no alternative to killing another human being—unless the alternative of allowing yet another to be killed seems acceptable.

I am not, in saying this, defending the right of governments to conscript people into their wars, nor am I denying that not enough time has been spent in urging non-violent alternatives to conflict at every level. The point is, rather, that there are times when non-violence simply doesn't work. It isn't, I realize, always meant to. As Gandhi insisted, at its best non-violence is not so much a strategy as a witness to truth—about yourself and about the life of the person who faces you as an enemy. But there may be circumstances when this does not seem morally possible, and at such times violence may seem—and may in fact be—the only moral alternative. Moral theology should not find ways to make these moments acceptable; they can be encountered only with fear, trembling, and profound repentance. The celebration of war, or of revolutionary violence, is obscene.

But another moral theology, one which simply denies the possibility that war and other forms of violence are ever anything other than exploitative or fearful responses to situations which could in every case be responded to non-violently, is dangerously naive.

If a non-violent response to evil works, that is nice, but it isn't the point. The point is that all human life has been revealed in Christ's incarnation as holy, even the lives of enemies and oppressors. This has nothing to do with the pacifism of those who think of Nazis or Communists as peace-loving sorts who would settle down and be good if only we didn't provoke them.

READING

16   GLOBAL MILITARISM

STOPPING THE WAR AGAINST THE THIRD WORLD

Michael T. Klare

Michael T. Klare is director of the Five College Program in Peace and World Security Studies based at Hampshire College in Amherst, Massachusetts.

Points to Consider:

1. Describe the concept of low-intensity conflict.

2. What is the "Great Fear"?

3. How does popular support of current government thinking enforce the "new perspective" on regional conflicts?

4. How does the Persian Gulf War reinforce the author's point of view? Be specific.

Michael T. Klare "Stopping the War Against the Third World," **The Progressive**, January, 1989. Reprinted by permission from **The Progressive**, 409 East Main Street, Madison, Wisconsin 53703.

105

Mankind is entering a period of increased social instability and faces the possibility of a breakdown of the global order as a result of a sharpening confrontation between the Third World and the industrial democracies.

For many years now, the peace movement has been preoccupied with one overwhelming threat: the risk of an Armageddon, an all-out nuclear conflict between the United States and the Soviet Union that virtually annihilates human society.

The improvement in relations between Washington and Moscow and the resumption of serious arms-control talks has significantly reduced the likelihood of a nuclear confrontation between the superpowers.

Because of President Reagan's virulent Cold War rhetoric and our own worries about nuclear conflict, we have tended to perceive all international conflict issues in East-West terms — in reference, that is, to the military competition between the United States and the Soviet Union. But the tempo of that competition has subsided and will, in all likelihood, continue to do so in the future. This is not the result of a change of heart by American officials, who remain as anti-communist as always. Rather, it is a product of the changing international economic environment.

While our political system does incorporate some suicidal tendencies, most top leaders of this country have come to understand the basic economic picture spelled out by such analysts as Paul Kennedy of Yale University, whose book, *The Rise and Fall of the Great Powers,* was an overnight sensation in 1988. Kennedy warns that hegemonic systems inevitably decline when their military expenditures exceed the carrying capacity of their economies. Most American leaders now acknowledge that we must diminish our investment in military spending to be able to devote additional resources to economic renewal. And because the U.S.-Soviet arms race is by far the most costly component of the military budget, that is where the cuts have to be made, and are being made.

Low Intensity Conflict

So far, so good. But there is a dark side to all of this: Having established a permanent peacetime security establishment to manage the Cold War, we are now saddled with a powerful military-industrial infrastructure that is not about

to disband itself voluntarily. One way to get at this problem is through economic conversion, which would provide incentives for industry and labor to switch from military to peacetime production. That will work—so long as we are talking about engineers and welders and machine-tool operators. But what do you do with people whose profession is systematic slaughter? How do you convert a tank gunner or an artilleryman or a bomber pilot?

I'm not sure that I have the answer. But, in any case, the military establishment has come up with its own answer: what is innocuously called "low-intensity conflict", or, in practice, war

> ## ILLEGITIMATE DEBTS
>
> *The peoples of the Third World, particularly in Latin America and the Philippines, are saying that. . .debts were contracted by illegitimate governments and should not be paid. [The money went for] weapons. It was not used for defense, but rather to repress and murder thousands of citizens.*
>
> Carol Barton, **CALC Report,** Summer 1988

against the hungry and angry and frustrated peoples of the Third World.

Low-intensity conflict, or LIC, is both a military strategy and a state of mind.

As a strategy, LIC affirms that American forces must be retrained and reconfigured to fight in the underdeveloped Southern Hemisphere against rebellious peasants and guerrilla armies. In practice, this means the "revitalization" of America's Special Operations Forces, the creation of four new "light infantry divisions" specifically configured for combat in the Third World, a one-third increase in the Navy's amphibious assault forces, a 100 percent increase in long-range airlift and sealift capabilities, and the creation of two new carrier battle groups and four surface action groups built around refurbished World War II-vintage battleships.

The total cost of this buildup, which has continued apace throughout the entire Reagan period, far exceeds total spending on "Star Wars" and other exotic nuclear programs. This effort has been accompanied, moreover, by stepped-up U.S. military exercises and deployments in Third World conflict areas, especially the Persian Gulf, the Mediterranean, the Indian Ocean, and the Caribbean.

These developments are worrisome enough, for they suggest a strategic realignment of massive proportions with unforeseeable consequences.

The Great Fear

But LIC also represents a reorientation of the military mindset. In essence, this outlook holds that the real threat to long-term American security lies in the South, across the Rio Grande, the Caribbean, the Mediterranean, the Indian Ocean. There, in the troubled and disordered regions of the Third World, America faces billions of disadvantaged people who seek a fairer share of the world's wealth. They produce much of the food and raw materials consumed in the North, and they no longer will settle for dismal poverty.

That is the "Great Fear," as John Gervasi once called it, and it both predates the Soviet scare and is coming to supersede it. The Pentagon recognizes the historical roots of this fear, tracing LIC doctrine back to the genocidal Indian Wars of the last century and to the equally genocidal Philippines Insurgency of 1898-1901, in which an estimated 600,000 Filipinos were shot or starved to death by American forces.

Of course, it is easy to submerge the Great Fear—the fear of rebellious Third World peoples—into the Soviet Scare and to portray them as one and the same, calling all Third World unrest a product of communist subversion. This propaganda tactic has been standard operating procedure during the Cold War. What is happening now, however, is a separation of the two fears into their component elements, with the Great Fear taking precedence over the Soviet Scare.

The primacy of LIC began to emerge in the 1970s, among military strategists who attempted to assess the "lessons" of Vietnam. Of particular importance was an influential 1977 Rand Corporation study, "Military Implications of a Possible World Order Crisis in the 1980s". This study suggested that "mankind is entering a period of increased social instability and faces the possibility of a breakdown of the global order as a result of a sharpening confrontation between the Third World and the industrial democracies." Because of the growing gap between rich and poor, "the North-South conflict . . . could get out of hand in ways comparable to the peasant rebellions that in past centuries engulfed large parts of Europe or Asia, spreading like uncontrollable prairie fires." And because only the United States has the capacity to fight these conflagrations, it will "be expected to use its military force to prevent the total collapse of the world order."

The new perspective surfaced again in the mid-1980s, when many younger military officers began to argue that the European-oriented build-up of the early 1980s had diverted U.S. policy-makers' attention from the mounting threat in the Third World.

The New Strategy

Advocating a Third World orientation would have been

considered heretical by most American policymakers only five years ago, but now it is becoming the conventional wisdom. With input from Henry Kissinger and Zbigniew Brzezinski, the U.S. Commission on Integrated Long-Term Strategy published a report entitled "Discriminate Deterrence" which sketches out the new strategy. The report argues that an "excessive focus" on "apocalyptic showdowns between the United States and the Soviet Union" has led to "tunnel vision among defense planners," diverting them "from trying to deal with many important and far more plausible [conflict] situations."

The "more plausible situations" envisioned by the Commission are revolts and regional conflicts in the Third World.

This view represents the core of elite U.S. thinking on military policy, cutting across the lines of both political parties. It will not, however, be expressed as a war against the have-nots of the Third World. Rather, it will be submerged in rhetoric about international terrorism, the drug trade, Third World disorder, the Islamic upheaval, and illegal immigration. Thus, when U.S. leaders speak of the threat posed by terrorism and drug trafficking, they are really expressing fear of "envious have-nots" who seek to confiscate our "national valuables."

If we look around us we can, I think, see many signs of this Great Fear. I see it in the prominence accorded to the Pledge of Allegiance issue in the Presidential campaign, in the popular idolization of Oliver North, in the success of "Rambo-type" movies, in the rage for war toys and camouflage gear among American youngsters, in efforts to seal off the U.S. border to Hispanic immigrants, in the approval given to President Reagan's April 1986 attack on Colonel Muammar Qaddafi's living quarters in Tripoli, and in the glee expressed by many Americans about the shootdown of an Iranian civilian airliner with 300 people aboard.

These impulses are strong, they are growing, and, so far as I can tell, they are not being actively resisted by the American peace movement.

Popular Support

The American people support efforts by the U.S. military to realign itself from an anti-Soviet to an anti-Third World force. Indeed, I would argue that the 1988 presidential campaign was largely a contest over who would be more forceful in battering down the troublemakers of the Third World when they next dare to challenge American interests.

What does it mean that our nation is gearing up to make war

on the Third World? It means, for the most part, fighting to protect entrenched oligarchies against the mass of the population. And it seems to me that you cannot preserve democracy and freedom and justice at home when you are fighting to preserve tyranny and exploitation and inequality abroad.

When you line up with those who rely on assassins and torturers to remain in power, you become part of the horror, even if you don't pull the trigger or switch on the electrodes.

When the American people fail to react in anger to an Administration that calls its overseas minions the "democratic resistance," when they permit the President to call torturers the "moral equivalent of the Founding Fathers," we should not be surprised or outraged to find our leaders subverting the U.S. Constitution, lying to Congress, breaking our laws, and conducting break-ins of citizen organizations. And that's just the beginning. If America continues to move in the direction I have sketched out, we can only assume that the corrosion and decay of our basic value system will accelerate.

Is this inevitable? No, not necessarily, but it surely is much more likely than a nuclear war. Indeed, if we ever do suffer a nuclear war, it will probably occur because of U.S. intervention in a small war, a low-intensity conflict, that escalates into a big war.

How do we resist the moral corrosion of our society? The first step obviously must be to examine these trends, and to make a commitment to engage them head on. Second, we must look into xenophobic and racist dimensions of the American psyche and search for methods to isolate and eradicate them. Until we begin to resist the tendency to view the world's have-nots as America's enemies, we will not be able to stem the revival of interventionism.

READING

17 GLOBAL MILITARISM

PREPARING TO WIN
LOW-INTENSITY CONFLICTS

David Silverstein

David Silverstein is a policy analyst for the Heritage Foundation in Washington D.C.

Points to Consider:

1. What is meant by low-intensity conflict?

2. Where will the most post-Cold War threats to U.S. security come from?

3. From the examples of historical low-intensity conflicts, match an incident with each method: gunboat diplomacy/covert actions/direct assistance/and occupation.

4. What steps should be taken, according to the author, to prepare the U.S. for future low-intensity conflicts?

David Silverstein, "Preparing America to Win Low-Intensity Conflicts," **Heritage Foundation Backgrounder,** August 31, 1990. Reprinted by permission of the Heritage Foundation.

America will continue to face severe challenges to its interests globally despite the improved relations with the Soviet Union.

While Americans may be ready to fight the Soviets in Europe or Iraqi forces in the Persian Gulf, this does not mean that America is ready to fight the much more limited battles against what is sure to be more typical threats of this decade: international terrorists, narcotics traffickers, revolutionary groups operating in the Third World, and assorted anti-American dictators.

Most of these threats will take the form of what national security experts call low-intensity conflict (LIC-pronounced "lick"), or hostile and frequently armed struggles ranging from psychological warfare and terrorist attacks to small scale wars. Though this danger grows, America lacks the manpower, equipment, organization, and has lacked the will to meet it.

What Is Low-Intensity Conflict?

Low-intensity conflict has been defined many ways. The White House defines it sparingly as ". . . conflict [that] involves the struggle of competing principles and ideologies below the level of conventional war. Poverty and the lack of political freedoms contribute to the instability that breeds such conflict."

A Reagan-era White House definition was more comprehensive: "low-intensity conflicts may be waged by a combination of means, including the use of political, economic, informational, and military instruments. . . .Major causes of low-intensity conflict are instability and lack of political and economic development in the Third World. These conditions provide fertile ground for unrest and for groups and nations wishing to exploit unrest for their own purposes. . . .An effective U.S. response to this form of warfare requires. . . the use of a variety of policy instruments among U.S. government agencies. Responses may draw on economic, political, and informational tools as well as military assistance."

Pentagon Definition—The Joint Chiefs of Staff of the military services define LIC as "political-military confrontation between contending states or groups below conventional war and above the routine, peaceful competition among states. It frequently involves protracted struggles of competing principles and ideologies. Low-intensity conflict ranges from subversion to the use of armed force. It is waged by a combination of means

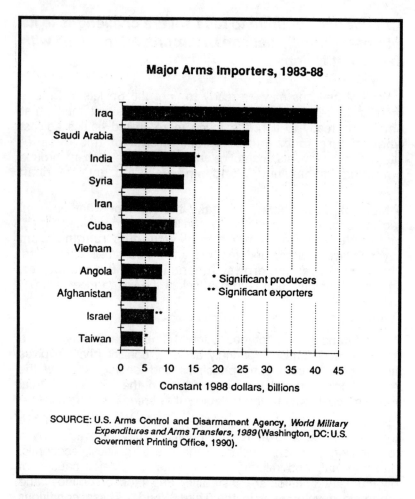

employing political, economic, informational, and military instruments. Low-intensity conflicts are often localized, generally in the Third World, but contain regional and global security implications."

The latter two definitions highlight important common points:
- the prevalence of LIC in the Third World;
- the importance of social, economic, and political factors in LIC; and
- the variety of informational, military, and economic tools that can be used to defeat an adversary in a LIC situation.

But these definitions also are lacking. LIC does not necessarily entail armed conflict. It can mean simply political

A SCARY THOUGHT

Suppose unrest and political problems in the Communist world allow nuclear weapons positioned in Warsaw Pact countries or rebellious republics of the Soviet Union to fall into the hands of revolutionaries? Whose finger would be on the trigger? A scary thought.

But even more ominous is the rapidly growing arms race in long-and intermediate-range missiles, nuclear and chemical warheads.

Highly unstable countries like Iraq, Iran, Libya, India, Syria, North Korea and Red China either have, or are attempting to build or buy, such weapons. Iraq and Iran have already used missiles and chemical weapons against each other's cities and installations in a war that has seen more than a million casualties.

In short, the most serious threat we face — from missiles — is rapidly growing worse.

Maj. Gen. Henry Mohr, **Human Events**, February 10, 1990

---

maneuvering and psychological warfare. It can be waged in the industrial as well as the Third World, as evidenced by such European terror groups as the Irish Republican Army (IRA) and the Basque Fatherland and Liberty group (ETA) in Spain.

Threats to U.S. Security

America continues to face many threats to its security and interests around the world. Though the Cold War is winding down, such dangers as international drug trafficking and insurgency warfare will continue, and most of them will arise in the Third World.

Latin America —

The U.S. has recognized Latin America as a vital security interest since proclamation of the Monroe Doctrine in 1823, which warned the European powers not to interfere in the affairs of the Western Hemisphere. Today, it is less the interference of outside hostile powers than narcotics production and trafficking that creates problems for the U.S. in Latin America. Two-thirds of the total illicit U.S. drug supply comes from Latin America, particularly from Bolivia, Colombia, and Peru. The production and flow of drugs, of course, not only damages American society, but can destabilize democratic governments through narco-terrorism (such as the random bombings by the Medellin drug cartel in Colombia) and related corruption. The laundering of illegal drug profits by legitimate banks further feeds corruption by making more funds available to the traffickers on both sides of the border.

Such Marxist guerrilla groups as the Farabundo Marti Liberation Front (FMLN) in El Salvador and Peru's Shining Path threaten their countries' democratically elected governments as well as U.S. political interests. The Shining Path has destabilized the government of Peru through terrorism and political assassination, and has forged links with coca growers, who supply the raw material for the manufacture of cocaine. The FMLN, which launched a major offensive against the Salvadoran government last winter, has unleashed waves of terror driving hundreds of thousands of Salvadorans out of their country.

Regional instability caused by insurgencies, terrorism, high national debts, inflation, and widespread poverty risks U.S. access to strategic minerals and markets in Latin America as well as thwarting U.S. attempts to promote democracy. Latin America's export of strategic materials to the U.S. include oil, bauxite (used to make aluminum) and antimony (important for making advanced metal alloys). The U.S. traded about $122 billion worth of goods with its Latin American neighbors in 1988.

Much of this trade passes not only through the Panama Canal, but also through the Caribbean Sea, which is potentially threatened by Cuba.

Asia —

Asia's greatest value to the U.S. is as a trading partner. Asia-U.S. trade in 1988 totaled over $280 billion. This includes raw materials that drive both Asian and U.S. industry as well as agricultural goods and such high-technology items as computer chips and electronics. Drug trafficking is a major problem across Asia. For one thing, it creates instability by corrupting governments and societies. For another, an increasing amount of opium entering the U.S. comes from the "Golden Triangle," formed by Burma, Laos, and Thailand, and from Afghanistan and Pakistan. Regional conflicts among Asian powers are another source of instability. The long simmering border conflict between Pakistan and India over the Kashmir region yet again is heating up. Growing Indian power is a threat to the traditional U.S. ally, Pakistan, which has served as the major conduit for U.S. supplies to the Afghan mujahideen. A potential danger in

Asia is rising Muslim fundamentalism. In Indonesia, which controls the sea lanes through which flows Middle East Oil on its way to Japan and the other industrial powers of East Asia, a fundamentalist-based mutiny was crushed this spring.

The Middle East—

As the Iraq-Kuwait crisis shows, the main U.S. interest in the Middle East is to assure a steady flow of oil to the industrialized world. Middle East oil accounted for 24.6 percent of total U.S. oil imports March, 1988. Middle East oil is even more important for U.S. allies in Europe and Asia. The total value of U.S. trade with the Middle East in 1988 was about $21 billion. Other major American interests in the area include the preservation of moderate, pro-Western states such as Egypt, Israel, Saudi Arabia, and Turkey as a hedge against the expansionary aims of Muslim fundamentalism and radical leaders like Iraq's Saddam Hussein. The U.S. also seeks to curtail the spread of nuclear, biological and chemical weapons and missile technology, eradicate terrorist groups, and halt the flow of opium and hashish from Lebanon.

Africa—

Though the U.S. traded only $15 billion worth of goods with Africa in 1988, the U.S. depends on Africa for over 85 percent of such critically important strategic metals as cobalt, chromium, and platinum group ores. These metals are used in jet engines and other high technology items and are needed to maintain America's technological and military superiority over the Soviet Union and other political adversaries. Africa controls such sea lanes as the Cape of Good Hope and the Horn of Africa, around which pass most oil shipments from the Middle East to America and Europe.

Low-Intensity Conflict in U.S. History

The first conflicts fought between American Indians and European settlers were low-intensity conflicts. So were the Boston Massacre in 1770 and the Boston Tea Party in 1773. The young U.S. dispatched Marines on Navy ships to what is today Tripoli, Libya, in 1804-1805, to protect American shipping from Barbary pirates and to rescue hostages. The last century's battles with American Indians employed what has been a familiar Soviet 20th century LIC technique: uprooting hostile populations to prevent them from aiding and abetting their forces in combat. This was the essence of the policy of Indian reservations.

Sixty LICs this century—Counter-insurgency operations in the Philippines from 1899 to 1913 against Filipino nationalist forces gave American troops their first taste of major jungle warfare. American has engaged in gunboat diplomacy, covert actions, direct assistance, occupation, and peacemaking actions throughout Latin America—in Bolivia, Brazil, Chile, Colombia, Cuba, Dominican Republic, El Salvador, the Falkland Islands, Guatemala, Mexico, Nicaragua, and Panama—and has kept European powers out of the Western Hemisphere in the 19th and 20th centuries. Operation "Just Cause" in Panama December, 1988, is the most recent example of U.S. military involvement in LIC. A study published in May, 1989 by the Congressional Research Service counts U.S. involvement in 60 LICs since 1899.

Policy failures—With its history of involvement in LIC, the U.S. should be well prepared to deal with it today. But resistance to fighting LIC or adopting an effective LIC policy exists throughout the federal bureaucracy. The focus of U.S. policy has always been elsewhere, particularly Western Europe, which seemed to pose the most overwhelming threat to U.S. interests. U.S. military and political strategies flowed from this assumption. Post-World War II U.S. defense policy was based on four requirements, all stemming from the Soviet threat:

1) deterrence based on nuclear and conventional strength;

2) forward deployment of U.S. military might on foreign territory;

3) alliances such as NATO; and

4) large standing and reserve forces. These have succeeded in winning the Cold War but have failed to address the problems of LIC.

Forging a New Policy

America faces serious challenges to its interests worldwide despite a weakened Soviet threat in Europe. These are not likely to subside in a world of nations divided by race and religion, led in many cases by heavily armed dictatorial regimes and suffering still from the effects of the decades-long Soviet effort to undermine global peace and stability. Rather, threats to America from low-intensity conflicts are apt to increase. Washington must reassess thoroughly its policy toward LIC if it is to deal with what is likely to be the most pervasive and frequent threat to American interests in the 1990s.

America is ill-prepared to deal with the low-intensity conflict threats to its global interests. Civilian and military leaders remain wedded to a war-planning and policy world view focused on East-West conflict in Europe, even as the Soviet military threat declines. This has hindered America's ability to tailor its resources to combat the threats to its security from those low-intensity conflicts like insurgency, terrorism, narcotics trafficking, and other types of limited warfare.

Meeting the Challenge—America will continue to face severe challenges to its interests globally despite the improved relations with the Soviet Union. Most of these challenges will not be from large military forces, such as those massed by Iraq on the Saudi border, but from low-intensity conflicts. America must be prepared meeting this LIC challenge. By defusing potential low-intensity conflicts before they break into armed warfare, and meeting them with military resistance if they do, America will not only protect its own interests, but enhance regional stability around the globe.

READING

18   GLOBAL MILITARISM

A NEW MILITARY BUDGET FOR A NEW WORLD

The Center for Defense Information

The Center for Defense Information supports an effective defense. It opposes excessive expenditures for weapons and policies that increase the danger of nuclear war. CDI believes that strong social, economic, political, and military components contribute equally to the nation's security. It was founded by retired high ranking military officers. The newsletter is called The Defense Monitor.

Points to Consider:

1. How has past military spending been justified?

2. Why have changes in the Soviet Union changed the needs for military spending?

3. How much should spending be reduced?

4. What kind of threats do Third World Nations present?

5. Describe the pressing economic, social, and environmental problems that confront our world.

"A New Military Budget for a New World," **The Defense Monitor**, Vol. XX, Number 2, 1991.

The United States could safely reduce annual military spending to some $200 billion within the next five to ten years.

For 45 years the threat posed to Western Europe by the Soviet Union and its Warsaw Pact allies was used to justify high levels of U.S. military spending. The collapse of the Warsaw Pact and the Soviet Union have essentially eliminated this threat.

As large and as costly as the U.S. deployment to the Persian Gulf has been, it does not approach the level of investment the U.S. has made over the past 45 years preparing for a possible war in Europe.

U.S. planners have traditionally assumed that a war in Europe would require 70 percent or more of U.S. conventional army, navy, and air forces. By comparison only about one-third of U.S. forces were sent to the Persian Gulf. Even this may have been considerably more than the U.S. would need to fight any other likely Third World adversary.

Thus, maintaining forces capable of fighting in the Third World need not prevent the U.S. from reaping substantial savings due to the Cold War's end. This is especially true since the Cold War military budget always included funds and forces for fighting wars in the Third World—to be fought, if necessary, at the same time as a larger war in Europe. Indeed, since 1979 the U.S. has specifically planned and budgeted for a possible war in the Persian Gulf.

The U.S. has been given a much needed opportunity to begin addressing the economic, social, and environmental problems that now pose the most serious threats to America's security. We cannot afford to squander this opportunity by continuing to pay for an enormous unneeded Cold War military establishment in a post-Cold War world.

Administration Plans

The Bush administration is asking for $291 billion for the Pentagon in 1992, compared to $286 billion for 1991. The Pentagon claims that when the effects of inflation are taken into account, next year's budget will actually represent a one percent decline from this year. In fact, when the Administration's $25 billion "supplemental" request to cover part of the cost of the war against Iraq is added, the latest budget request clearly represents an increase in military spending.

According to the Administration's latest five-year plan,

spending will reach $298 billion by 1996. Again, it argues that when inflation is taken into account this will actually represent a 14 percent decline. Such a reduction, even if real, falls far short of the level of cuts the U.S. can now safely afford to make.

In reality, by making larger cuts in force structure and reducing the rate at which existing weapons are replaced by more expensive ones, the U.S. could safely reduce annual military spending to some $200 billion within the next five to ten years.

> ## NO MORE IRAQS
>
> *No other Third World country that the U.S. might plausibly face in coming years is as strong as Iraq was at the start of the Persian Gulf War. None of these countries is capable of successfully challenging the far larger and more effective forces that the U.S. has today and will have tomorrow.*
>
> **Pre-War**
>
> | | Iraq | Libya | Syria | Cuba | N. Korea | Iran | USA |
> |---|---|---|---|---|---|---|---|
> | Manpower* | 1,000 | 85 | 404 | 181 | 1,111 | 504 | 2,050 |
> | Tanks | 5,500 | 2,300 | 4,000 | 1,100 | 3,500 | 500 | 16,150 |
> | Aircraft | 800 | 513 | 558 | 185 | 716 | 185 | 7,150 |
>
> *Manpower in thousands.
>
> Chart prepared by Center for Defense Information

Nuclear Forces

Spending on nuclear forces is perhaps the clearest area where cuts can and should be made to reflect the demise of the U.S.-Soviet military competition. The Soviet Union has already agreed to large cuts in nuclear forces as part of the Strategic Arms Reduction Treaty. It has also stopped or begun to slow the production of new nuclear weapon systems such as the Typhoon-class missile submarine, the Blackjack bomber, and the SS-24 intercontinental ballistic missile (ICBM).

Preparing for possible future wars in the Third World provides no justification for the enormous U.S. nuclear arsenal. Some Third World countries may develop and build small nuclear forces within the next five to ten years. But the U.S. could completely destroy any such country with a tiny fraction of the 12,000 long-range nuclear weapons it has today.

Presently the U.S. spends about $65 billion a year on nuclear forces. This includes the costs of developing, producing, and operating the weapons and delivery systems plus costs associated with the communications, logistics, and other facilities needed to support these weapon systems. Given recent changes, the U.S. could reduce annual spending on nuclear forces to perhaps $25 billion by 1995.

The Persian Gulf War

The countries of the Third World do not pose a military challenge to the U.S. that is even remotely comparable to that posed in the past by the Warsaw Pact. The U.S. enjoys close economic and positive political relations with the vast majority of countries in the Third World.

Of the handful of Third World countries that have had mixed or hostile relations with the U.S. in the past, pre-war Iraq—with some 800 combat aircraft and 5,500 tanks—was probably the strongest. Nevertheless, using only about one-third of its ground and air forces, the U.S. was able to defeat Iraq in a six-week war.

No More Iraqs

If the war with Iraq cannot justify a Cold War-sized military budget, certainly no other Third World threat can plausibly do so.

The only Third World country with military forces clearly larger than those of pre-war Iraq is China. U.S. planners have not considered the possibility of war with China a serious prospect since the 1970s. Indeed, the U.S. has cultivated economic, political, and even limited military ties to China for more than a decade.

Gulf War Costs

Estimates for the cost of the war against Iraq range from about $45 billion to $70 billion. This year the Administration has asked for $15 billion, on top of the $2 billion it received last year, to begin paying these costs. This "supplemental" appropriation is over and above its $291 billion request for the 1992 military budget. Although U.S. allies pledged some $54 billion to cover the cost of the war, as of early April 1991 they had made only about $31 billion in payments. If these other payments fail to materialize, the Administration will need to request additional funds.

Other Challenges

If the U.S. faced no pressing economic, social, and environmental problems, then excessive military spending might not be a problem. But in fact the U.S. faces enormous challenges in these areas.

The U.S. economy is increasingly losing ground to foreign

competition. One reason for this is the U.S. federal deficit, which is expected to reach nearly $300 billion in 1991. Cuts in military spending could contribute significantly to the reduction of the federal deficit. Reducing the size of the deficit would in turn free up money that could then be spent improving U.S. industry to make it more competitive.

There is also no shortage of social or environmental problems which need to be addressed. Cuts in wasteful military spending could allow the U.S. to make needed increases in spending on education, for example, or help pay the $300 billion it is expected to cost to clean up U.S. military bases and nuclear weapons facilities.

The five-year budget agreement reached in 1990 stipulates that any savings from cutting military spending must go first toward reducing the federal deficit. However, the budget agreement's separate caps on domestic and military spending are replaced with a single overall cap in fiscal years 1994 and 1995. It would then be possible to shift savings from the military directly into needed social and environmental programs without breaking the budget agreement.

Finally, money saved by cutting military spending could be used to reduce U.S. dependence on foreign oil. If the U.S. spent as much money on conservation and developing alternative energy resources as it does on maintaining forces for fighting in the Persian Gulf, it might well be able to eliminate any dependence on foreign oil.

Budget savings can be made both by cutting the size of U.S. forces and slowing the rate at which U.S. forces are equipped with new weapons. By making such cuts the U.S. should be able to reduce annual military spending from $286 billion in 1991 to approximately $200 billion in 1995. A positive and manageable step in this direction would be to reduce the 1992 military budget from the $291 billion requested to $266 billion. Done wisely, this first "peaceful dividend" would pave the way for more significant reductions in future year.

Conclusion

- Planned U.S. arms sales will increase the chances of conflict in the Third World and could make U.S. involvement in such wars more likely.

- Maintaining the capability to destroy the Soviet Union completely with nuclear weapons does not require that the U.S. buy a single new B-2 bomber.

- The Pentagon is proposing out of date Cold War spending levels at a time when the U.S. faces critical economic, social, and environmental problems which post significant threats to U.S. security.

- The U.S. could reduce military spending from $286 billion this year to $200 billion in 1995 and still fulfill all essential military requirements.

READING

19 GLOBAL MILITARISM

THE HIGH COST OF ARMS REDUCTION

Malcolm Wallup

Malcolm Wallop is a U.S. Senator from Washington and is a member of the Armed Services Committee.

Points to Consider:

1. How does the author describe the "peace dividend"?

2. How does he describe the Soviet Union?

3. What is the Strategic Defense Initiative (SDI)?

4. How is the Soviet threat related to SDI?

5. Why is space important in a military sense?

Senator Malcolm Wallup, "Congress Forgets the Meaning of Defense," **The Wall Street Journal.** Reprinted with permission of **The Wall Street Journal.** © 1990 Dow Jones & Company, Inc. All rights reserved.

Congress is overlooking the high price of un-preparedness in its zeal to spend the peace dividend—before there is a dividend, and before there is true and certain peace.

The U.S. Defense Department is, of course, certainly not entitled to a blank check. Reasonable cuts in defense spending are the necessary response to the world's changing military and political situation, and to our own deficit woes. But the Pentagon is not a cash cow to be milked to nourish a bloated welfare state. Its mission is to safeguard our freedom by keeping our military forces strong and ready.

Military Unpreparedness

Take a look at history. Every time the U.S. has embarked on a drastic unilateral reduction in military capability for a short-term gain, the ultimate result has been a high cost—in American blood as well as treasure.

We were woefully unprepared when we entered World War I. Recruits drilled with broomsticks instead of rifles, and the U.S. had to borrow artillery, tanks and aircraft from the French and British. In the 1930s, isolationism gave us a weak military. With Pearl Harbor, we learned the cost. U.S. submarines went to war with torpedoes that would not explode on contact. Our aviators and their obsolete aircraft were shot down in scores by Japanese pilots flying modern Zeros. After World War II, the lesson repeated itself. The U.S. demobilized precipitously and announced that it had no security interest in East Asia. The result was the North Korean invasion of South Korea 40 years ago this summer, and the death of 50,000 Americans.

Congress today is overlooking the high price of unpreparedness in its zeal to spend the peace dividend—before there is a dividend, and before there is true and certain peace.

Legislation in the Senate also stopped modernization of ICBMs (Intercontinental Ballistic Missiles). There is no strategic rationale for these steps. The process that produced the legislation was not a thoughtful exercise in defense policy analysis, but an accountant's exercise. The very term "peace dividend" is the language of accountants. So it should come as no surprise that Congress is acting with little consideration of specific threats, strategic imperatives or military requirements. The result is strategy made by bookkeepers.

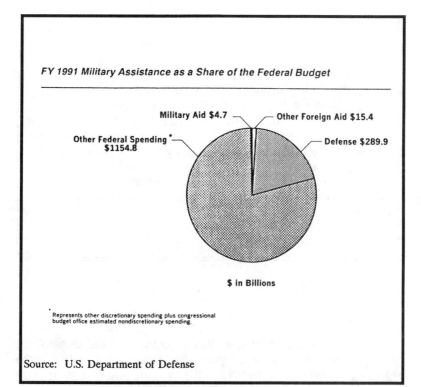

Source: U.S. Department of Defense

Strategic Defense

The most glaring example of the triumph of short-term politics over sound defense policy is the attitude toward strategic programs, space and the Strategic Defense Initiative (SDI).

In a trip to Lawrence Livermore National Laboratory, President Bush said, "In the 1990s, strategic defense makes more sense than ever before." But the Senate Armed Services Committee authorized nearly a billion dollars less than the president's SDI request. The House Armed Services Committee proposes to cut SDI by nearly $2 billion.

There are worse prospects for SDI than reduced funding. An amendment to the Senate defense bill would radically restructure SDI. This comes at the moment when the program stands on the threshold of producing concrete benefits. By cutting $400 million from Phase I of SDI and "brilliant pebbles," the most promising near-term technology, the amendment would foreclose the deployment of an actual defense system, and steer SDI toward long-term, open-ended research. The senators would sacrifice the Defense Department's freedom to manage the

---

THE RUSH TO DISARM

The headlines tell the story: "Defense Secretary Cheney: Cut $180 Billion from Military." "U.S. Studies Even Deeper Troop Cuts." "Air Force May Clip Its Wings." In Washington, a leading conservative columnist said, "We can quit arming." And a front-page report in the Wall Street Journal *was headlined: "Coming Home: Warsaw Pact's Disarray Could Finally Slash U.S. Forces in Europe." The question now seems to be not whether to cut America's defenses—rebuilt at great cost and effort in the first half of the last decade—but how soon and by how much. The stampede to disarm seems irresistable.*

America's Future newsletter, January 1990, p. 1.

---

program efficiently.

National Debate

Senator Nunn has predicted that a "broad national debate" on strategic defense will result from this amendment. He's quite right. The American people will have the chance to decide whether they want SDI to become a technological welfare program, or whether they want to get any return—in the form of an actual defense—from the six years and nearly $20 billion invested in SDI. They must decide through their elected representatives whether to ensure by law that SDI will never produce any real security and will instead become merely another expensive entitlement program.

Ironically, scientists and engineers working on SDI don't favor pure research either. They, too, hope for a usable product.

Building on the steady and dramatic technical progress to date, and under the Strategic Defense Initiative Organization's new director, Henry Cooper, there is the real possibility that SDI funds will be spent to build the protection that the American people think they have been paying for all along.

If we turn our backs on SDI, we're not just rejecting the option of defense against ballistic missiles. SDI also means progress in the critical arena of space. It is significant that the Senate defense bill would also terminate the MILSTAR space-based command and control program, and that Sens. John Kerry (D., Mass.) and Tom Harkin (D., Iowa) want to kill off our anti-satellite capability as well.

As long as there is conflict between competing interests and ideologies, space will not be exempt from it. Indeed, we are entering an era when space control is becoming the crucial military leverage, and may determine the course of future conflicts—without a shot ever being fired by terrestrial forces.

Military forces have historically opened the way into new frontiers of human endeavor, whether it was navies opening up the high seas, or, as in our own history, the Army exploring the new Western frontier, and providing security for settlers, homesteaders and railroads.

There is no reason the development of the space frontier should not follow the same pattern. The military's initial investment and sustained operations in space will push technology forward, bring down the cost of launching and keeping platforms in orbit, and provide the nucleus of future settlements and commercial ventures. As in the past, "trade will follow the flag."

Via SDI to Space

The first step toward the essential mastery of space is SDI, the greatest technical and strategic innovation of the past quarter century. A strategic defense system will greatly reduce the military utility or blackmail potential of nuclear-armed ballistic missiles. But SDI will give us more than just a missile defense. It will also lead the way to U.S. dominance in the ultimate high ground of space, and the "high seas" of the future.

The list of civil and commercial as well as military benefits to be gained from space is endless. But the investments will be, shall we say, astronomical. Can we expect businesses to risk huge investments in space unless their security is reasonably assured, unless U.S. interests in space can be defended as they are on the earth's surface? If congressional leaders, especially leaders of the armed services committees, allow Congress to forestall the immeasurable advantages of a space-based strategic defense, then their pretensions to the role of strategist ring hollow.

As Congress takes up action on the defense bill, the American people need to remind their representatives that American moral strength, political resolve, military capability and technical prowess over the past 40 years have brought us to the threshold of victory. When we are so close to seeing the end of Soviet imperialism, the dividend ought to be more than a transitory or illusory peace. By our continued resolve, peace, when it comes, will be genuine and lasting.

READING

20   GLOBAL MILITARISM

IMPOVERISHED BY RUNAWAY ARMS RACE

Christian Social Action

Points to Consider:

1. What is the Harvest of Peace?

2. Summarize the main theme of the resolution.

3. How would the U.S. gain by adopting such a policy? How would the Third World nations benefit?

4. Why does the author believe that national defense has been excessive?

Excerpted from an article entitled "Share the Harvest of Peace," **Christian Social Action,** May, 1990.

There is no excuse for hunger, only a lack of public outrage and political will.

A Harvest of Peace Resolution was introduced in 1990 in Congress by Senator Mark Hatfield (R-OR) and Representative Matt McHugh (D-NY). The resolution goes beyond the administration's budget proposal by addressing the historic opportunity to provide a "peace dividend" to help meet basic human needs.

The Harvest of Peace Resolution calls for the nations of the world to reduce military spending by half by the year 2000 and redirect resources toward ending hunger. The resolution also calls for reduced military assistance to developing nations, as regional conflicts are one of the primary causes of hunger.

"There is no excuse for hunger, only a lack of public outrage and political will," said Art Simon, president of Bread for the World, a grassroots movement against hunger, which is campaigning in support of the Harvest of Peace Resolution. "Democracy was a strong enough force to tear down the Berlin Wall; it can also be strong enough to dismantle the 'pork barrel barricade' in Congress which protects our excessive defense budget."

While Congress has increased defense spending during a time of peace and rapidly fading communist threats, effective human needs programs have been cut or ignored. For example, the Head Start program reaches only 20 percent of those eligible. The Special Supplemental Food Program for Women, Infants and Children (WIC) reaches only 50 percent of eligible high-risk mothers and children; and job training for low-income people reaches only 6 percent of those who need preparation to enter the job market.

"The national defense of this nation has left us vulnerable, but not because we lack an arsenal," said Sen. Hatfield. "Our vulnerability today is a nonproductive and noncompetitive economy. Our vulnerability is the people who are without homes, nutrition, education and health care."

The Resolution

It is the sense of the Congress that the United States should help achieve common security by reducing the world's reliance on the military and redirecting resources to peaceful efforts toward overcoming hunger and poverty and meeting basic human needs by:

GUNS VS. GRAIN

Food and weapons are among the items seemingly most fundamental to our world. They are rightly seen as symbols of the extremes of human existence: the first sustaining life, the second destroying it.

At first sight, it is tempting to contrast arms and grain trade by regarding one as objectionable and the other as desirable. Arms can legitimately be seen as the bearers of death and destruction. And, since they add nothing to a nation's productive capacity, arms waste precious resources. That is particularly true in countries where even the most basic of needs — adequate clothing, housing and nourishment — are simply unobtainable for the majority of the population.

But neither is growing agricultural trade necessarily a blessing. Rising grain imports are often a testament to a country's inability to feed itself, implying a dangerous reliance on foreign supplies.

Michael G. Renner, **World Watch,** Mar./Apr. 1989

1. Negotiating agreements with the Soviet Union for substantial and verifiable reduction in overall military forces and spending, and urging other nations to reduce their military forces and spending, with the goal of halving worldwide military spendings by the year 2000;

2. Reducing military assistance and arms sales to developing nations and urging other nations to do likewise;

3. Encouraging peaceful settlement of conflicts through regional and international negotiations.

4. Providing increased assistance to developing nations to overcome hunger and poverty, to reduce debt burdens, to promote human rights and people's participation in political decisions affecting them, to ensure sustainable development, and to protect the environment;

5. Increasing support domestically for programs that address human needs;

6. Helping defense industries and their employees convert to productive nondefense work; and

7. Reducing the federal deficit.

If the costs of military spending victimize poor hungry people, the consequences of military spending make matters even worse. In nations such as Ethiopia, Sudan, and El Salvador, regional conflicts fueled by military aid from the superpowers have destroyed the people's ability to raise and distribute food. In Mozambique and Angola, nearly 9 million people are at risk of starvation, not because of drought or famine, but because of fields, roads, bridges and entire villages destroyed by rebels receiving outside military aid.

"The world would be a safer place," said Simon, "if we stopped arming ourselves and our allies to the teeth and began to address the lack of food, shelter and human rights which cause people to go to war. The United States would be a stronger and more secure nation with a healthier economy, less hunger and poverty, and without a $2.9 trillion national debt which was created in part by our massive military buildup."

Bread for the World's campaign to "Share the Harvest of Peace" is projected to be a three-year, multimillion dollar effort involving local churches, most religious denominations, and a wide variety of human needs, peace and social justice organizations. *Sane/Freeze Campaign for Global Security, World Hunger Year, Interfaith Action for Economic Justice,* and the *Coalition on Human Needs* were among the first organizations to endorse the resolution.

Bread for the World is a national grassroots movement of Christians that seeks justice for the hungry people in the United States and throughout the world. Bread for the World's 40,000 members are organized by congressional districts to lobby their members of Congress to support measures which can help hungry people.

READING

21   GLOBAL MILITARISM

THIS IS NO TIME TO BEAT OUR SWORDS INTO PLOWSHARES

Thomas Sowell

Thomas Sowell is a columnist for Scripps Howard News Service. Sowell is a former professor of economics at UCLA, and has also worked for the U.S. Department of Labor. He is now a senior fellow with the Hoover Institution on War Revolution and Peace at Stanford University.

Points to Consider:

1. What are the dangerous illusions mentioned by the author?

2. How can trouble in the Third World threaten U.S. security?

3. Describe the author's "history lesson".

4. What is the "polio fallacy"?

Thomas Sowell "Our Own Illusions Threaten Our Future," **Conservative Chronicle,** February 21, 1990. Reprinted by permission of **Scripps Howard News Service.**

The reduced danger of a land war in Europe has been taken by many as a sign that we can take an axe to our military budget and use the savings to set up more federal give-away programs.

Many countries face grim realities that threaten their future. The United States is fortunate enough to have the material resources and the technology to handle the realities. It is our own illusions that threaten our future.

Dangerous Illusions

Our most dangerous illusions are about military necessities. People are looking for the "peace dividend" the way a small child looks for Santa Claus. The reduced danger of a land war in Europe has been taken by many as a sign that we can take an axe to our military budget and use the savings to set up more federal give-away programs.

Many politicians who talk this way have also been claiming for years to be concerned about the federal deficit and our record national debt. Yet they are itching to start another spending spree, instead of using any savings in military spending to reduce the national debt.

Before we beat our swords into plowshares and our missiles into food stamps, we need to recognize that a land war in Europe with the Warsaw Pact countries was only one of many military contingencies we had to counter. The Soviet Union still has the largest arsenal of nuclear missiles ever assembled. The Middle East could erupt at any time and we have probably not heard the last of Central America.

More important than any specific danger is the bitter fact that military preparedness has been the price of peace and survival for thousands of years. Our intelligentsia talk as if the Cold War was the only reason we needed military defense. After years of treating the Cold War as if it were some kind of psychological problem, they are all too eager to declare it over and done with—and to start disarming.

What if someday someone like Libya's Qadaffi manages to get his hand on two or three nuclear missiles and launches them at New York or Los Angeles? Wouldn't a "Star Wars" defense system turn out to be well worth the cost if it could shoot these missiles down out over the Atlantic?

The argument against nuclear defense systems has been that the Soviet Union could launch enough missiles to overwhelm

> ## SLASHING DEFENSE
>
> *Allow me to suggest that the world isn't coming to anything new; it's where it's always been. There are responsible powers—like us—and blatantly malicious ones—like Iraq. The job of the responsible powers, from ancient Rome through imperial Britain on up to post-World War II America, has been to make sure the malicious ones don't embroil or infect the world outside their borders. The world, like any urban jungle, needs policemen. At this moment the badge and truncheon are ours by default.*
>
> *Slashing the defense budget, as opposed to rearranging it to meet an evolving situation, is bad enough. Gutting programs needed to deal with neighborhood thugs like Saddam Hussein is idiotic.*
>
> William Murchison, **Conservative Chronicle**, August 22, 1990, p. 1.

any system. Whether or not that was true, a period of diminished threat from the USSR and a spread of nuclear capability to smaller nations means that nuclear defense makes more sense than ever.

It will of course cost money—money that politicians would rather hand out as goodies from the "peace dividend".

Too much discussion of military defense is based on the kind of fallacy that cost needless lives from polio. After polio vaccines brought that killer disease under control, many people eventually decided that the danger was past and stopped getting themselves or their children vaccinated. A resurgence of polio brought more crippling and death.

History Lesson

After nearly half a century of maintaining U.S. military forces at a level that made a major war too costly for anyone to start, many people now think that being free of a major war all that time proves that huge military spending was unnecessary. They want to stop doing the very thing that produced peace.

This fallacy is not peculiar to the United States or to our time. Great nations whose wealth and power have given them peace have often decided to skimp on power so that they could enjoy more of their wealth. It happened in the last centuries of the Roman Empire, in China during the Ming dynasty, and in the Ottoman Empire as it began its long decline.

Internal social degeneracy of various sorts accompanied these complacent neglects of military defense. Each of these seemingly invincible empires paid the price as other nations took advantage of their self-imposed weakness to inflict devastating defeats on them.

Great Britain narrowly escaped the same fate. At one time, Britain reigned supreme as the unchallenged superpower of the world. They deliberately maintained a navy larger than the next two largest navies in the world. Military defense burdens on the British taxpayers were the largest per capita in the world.

Eventually, the British decided that they couldn't keep this up. It is not clear that they really saved any money, when you count the cost of having to fight two World Wars in this century.

Some say that the only thing you learn from history is that people don't learn anything from history. We can only hope that the "polio fallacy" doesn't become rampant as Washington politicians try to cut a big "peace dividend" out of the defense budget.

Peace is itself a dividend. It is dangerous to become greedy for more.

READING

22   GLOBAL MILITARISM

EXPOSING THE ROOTS OF MILITARISM

Roger Powers

Roger Powers wrote this article in his capacity as the Clergy and Laity Concerned's Militarism Program Coordinator. Powers has several years experience in the peace and justice movement and has pursued graduate studies in international relations at the University of Denver.

Points to Consider:

1. How is militarism defined?

2. What is meant by "civil religion"?

3. How does racism lead to militarism?

4. How does current national security ideology actually make citizens less secure?

5. Why is peace related to justice?

Roger Powers, "Exposing the Roots of Militarism," **CALC Report,** March/April, 1986.

Around the world it is the people of color who have borne the brunt of militarism.

Broadly defined, militarism is thinking which prescribes military solutions to social and economic problems. It creates a society, infused with military symbols and ideals, in which violence or the threat of violence is the pervasive form of power.

Examples of militarism in our society are all around us, from the way our nation relates to other nations to the way individual members of a family relate to one another. When a U.S.-supported Third World government is faced with popular revolt, the U.S. responds with additional military aid and sometimes with direct military intervention to maintain the unjust status quo. Similarly, when riots break out in U.S. cities because people are unemployed and do not have adequate food, housing, and health care, the National Guard is called in to "keep the peace." Crime is combatted, not by building a more just society in which everybody's basic needs are met but by putting more police out onto the streets. An ailing national economy is given a shot in the arm by increasing the military budget and awarding more contracts to the defense industry. Teen unemployment, especially high among young people of color, is reduced through military recruitment in the high schools and through the "poverty draft". In the home, family members who have difficulty communicating with one another often resort to violence, spouse and/or child abuse. Even the movies our children watch and the toys they play with glorify military power and violence, the "Rambo" movies and the Coleco Industries' Rambo doll being just two examples.

The Malady Within Our Spirit

Militarism and its underlying causes were what Martin Luther King, Jr. was referring to when he said that "the war in Vietnam is but a symptom of a far deeper malady within the American spirit." He recognized that how we act as a nation is deeply rooted in the values we hold and called for a "radical revolution of values" in the United States.

In the past, the peace movement has tried to stop the nuclear arms race either by seeking to prevent the development and/or deployment of weapons systems or by advocating a nuclear weapons freeze. For the most part these efforts have been unsuccessful. Why? Because fundamental values associated with anti-Sovietism, the powerful profit motive of the military-industrial complex, and national security ideology, have

not been directly challenged. Similarly, the peace movement has put a lot of energy into countering U.S. intervention in Third World countries. But these efforts, too, have had little impact because the basic assumption that the U.S. has the right to do virtually anything it wants to anywhere in the world has not been significantly undermined.

U.S. militarism is rooted in the values promoted by American "civil religion". Civil religion promotes the understanding that as U.S. citizens, we are God's "chosen people" living in "the

WAR TAX RESISTANCE

Pennsylvania was founded by William Penn for religious liberty. Penn believed, and so did the early settlers, that to create a Quaker colony meant there would be no militia, no war taxes and no oaths. These were conceived to be part of religious freedom, and in the early years of Pennsylvania, there was no militia, and there were no war taxes and no oaths. At first, the Pennsylvania Assembly refused to levy any taxes for the direct carrying on of war. Instead. . .there would be almost a noncombat status for Quaker money. It could be used to provide foodstuffs to be used to feed the Indians, or it could purchase grain or relieve sufferings. It would not be used to provide guns and gunpowder.

Religious freedoms preceded and are incorporated into the federal government. Pennsylvania was founded for religious freedom, and religious freedom meant no taxes for war, no militia service, and the right of affirmation. Friends think that the federal government incorporated part of that understanding in the affirmation clause in the constitution, in the first amendment, and in the religion clauses in the Pennsylvania Constitution. Friends think that the government has in good faith tried to accommodate us in our position on military service, and what Friends are wanting from the government now is a like accommodation on a subject which is the same to us as conscientious objection: the paying of taxes which will be used to create weapons to threaten and to kill.

J. William Frost, **Friends Journal,** March 1988

---

promised land" and that therefore God is on our side. Our nation's tremendous wealth is considered God's blessing upon us for being faithful, hardworking people. Likewise, the poverty in the Third World is ascribed to the laziness of the Third World poor. When we go to war, we fight for "God and Country" against enemies whom we describe as Godless, evil, even Satanic. U.S. warfighting thus takes on the character of a Holy crusade. (In this regard, it is not insignificant that President Reagan's infamous speech in which he described the Soviet Union as the "Evil Empire" was given before a group of religious broadcasters, for it is the "electronic church" that is being used by elements of the Religious Right to preach civil religion to millions.

Racism

Racism and militarism have been integrally related throughout American history. The early European settlers engaged in genocidal acts against native peoples who they regarded as "savages." Militias were organized to take care of the "Indian problem" and to defeat slave uprisings. Paramilitary groups—lynching parties and later the Ku Klux Klan—used terror tactics to subdue the African-American population. And in the 1950s and 60s, when people of color took to the streets to demand their civil rights, the White establishment responded with fire hoses, tear gas, police dogs and billy clubs.

Around the world it is the people of color who have borne the brunt of militarism. From the end of the 19th century to the present day, most incidences of U.S. military intervention have occurred in the Third World. Indeed, intervention is rationalized by the racist view that Third World peoples are not competent enough to govern themselves or determine their own destinies.

The development of nuclear weapons has also taken its toll on Third World communities. In Native American communities where uranium is mined and in the Pacific where nuclear warheads are tested, people of color are being exposed to abnormally high amounts of radiation and are suffering ill health as a result.

Racism is also a fundamental part of militarism in that it provides a basis for dehumanizing the enemy. The dehumanization process is essential in conditioning an individual soldier to kill or preparing an entire country to wage war.

Materialism

"What causes wars, and what causes fightings among you? Is it not your passions that are at war in your members? You desire and do not have; so you kill. And you covet and cannot obtain; so you fight and wage war." (James 4:1-2) These words from the letter of James speak of an age old truth: that wars are often caused by desire, by the drive to possess territory, natural resources, or some other form of material wealth. It was this drive which brought European explorers and settlers to the New World and which made the original thirteen colonies expand and eventually grow to become a dominant world power.

The extent of U.S. materialism is evidenced by the fact that the U.S. consumes 30 to 40 percent of the world's resources, while comprising only 6 percent of the world's population. In order to amass such wealth, and then to protect it, a powerful military was necessary. The U.S. armed forces enabled the U.S. to expand its influence beyond its borders and gain access to and control of more land and mineral resources, cheap labor and new markets. Today, the protection of these U.S. national interests abroad requires massive military power on a global scale.

National Security Ideology

Many U.S. government policies, even those which are unjust or those which obstruct peace and justice, have been justified in terms of U.S. "national security". (These policies range from the repression of civil liberties at home to the sponsorship of dictators abroad.) But like the proverbial sacred cow, what constitutes U.S. "national security" is neither spelled out nor questioned; it is just blindly accepted.

Ironically, U.S. foreign and domestic policies which purport to enhance U.S. "national security", are actually making millions of U.S. citizens (not to mention the rest of the world) less and less secure. Like the homeowner who continually adds roofing to his house to protect it from the elements, only to have the entire structure collapse from the extra weight, the U.S. is destined for collapse if it continues to prop up the unjust status quo with its economic power and military might.

The prophets told us that a nation's ultimate security rests in its covenant with God. For example, in the book of Jeremiah, when the people of Judah sought God's refuge in a time of national crisis, Jeremiah urged the nation to first repent of its sins and then to do justice—welcoming the stranger, feeding the hungry, clothing the naked, sheltering the homeless. Only then would Judah find security in God.

The wisdom of the prophets still holds true today. Nuclear weapons and rapid deployment forces do not make our nation more secure. On the contrary, we will only be secure to the extent that we promote justice throughout the world, seeing to it that the basic needs of all people are met.

READING

23

GLOBAL MILITARISM

LIVING IN A DANGEROUS WORLD

A. M. Gray

General A. M. Gray made the following statement before the House Committee on Armed Services.

Points to Consider:

1. Why does the author believe the U.S. is a world leader?

2. How will the U.S. maintain this position of world leader?

3. What two elements contribute to domestic and international instability?

4. With less available funding, how will the U.S. provide an adequate defense for its people?

Excerpted from testimony by General A. M. Gray before the House Committee on Armed Services, March 14, 1990.

146

The majority of the crises we have responded to since the end of World War II have not directly involved the Soviet Union.

Any discussion of our national requirement for military forces for the approaching decades must include an examination of the international and domestic environment, our national interests, existing and anticipated threats, technology, our national strategy, and future force structure requirements. The world has entered again into an era of dynamic and exciting change. Quite understandably, our citizens and warriors are optimistic about more enduring and peaceful relationships throughout the world. There also is much uncertainty with regard to the future security environment of the coming decades. Our nation must reevaluate its military force requirements in light of the changing threat, our national goals and interests, evolving strategy, and diminishing defense resources. As we pass through this period of transition, we must not lose sight of the fact that in the present environment of uncertainty, the United States remains the keystone of international stability. Our position as a world leader is the direct result of our unrelenting commitment to democratic ideals, our economic power, and our willingness to maintain credible military force levels to protect our interests and those of our friends. Put another way, the people of our great nation continue to demand that we maintain our status as a superpower. If we are to maintain this status well into the next century, we must have a balance among all the elements of national power.

International Environment

A nation's intentions, capabilities, and interests may change, but geography and enduring national values do not. The United States has been and will continue to be a maritime nation with global economic and political interests. Our basic national security interests and objectives will remain constant. The preservation of a stable world environment through the maintenance of credible military forces and strong alliances will remain crucial to our survival as a nation and our political and economic well being.

The changing nature of the Soviet Union and the emergence of new regional powers and threats will be the greatest source of change and uncertainty in the world. In a very short time, we have witnessed dramatic developments in the international security environment. Emerging changes in the Soviet Union

Pact threat are causing us to redefine the way we and our allies view the world. The scope of these developments are not yet fully understood. Accordingly, there is a need to proceed with both caution and vision. In light of the changing threat, we have begun, and will continue, to reduce those forces focused on the Soviet threat. It is premature to undertake a widespread restructuring of our general purpose and special operation capable forces, the core of our crisis response capability, without a clearer assessment of the long term effect of the ongoing changes within the Soviet Union and Eastern Europe on international stability and a better understanding of the new world order emerging in the previous lesser developed regions of the world In spite of the uncertainty surrounding the changes occurring, one thing is certain: no longer will we have the luxury of focusing the majority of our defense efforts on a single threat or a single region of the world.

The international security environment is in the midst of changing from a bipolar balance to a multipolar one with polycentric dimensions. The restructuring of the international environment has the potential to create regional power vacuums which could result in instability and conflict. We cannot permit these voids to develop either through disinterest, benign neglect, or lack of capability. If we are to maintain our position as a world leader, and protect our interests, we must be capable of and willing to protect our global interests. This requires that we maintain our capability to respond to likely regions of conflict.

Growing economic power will, in some regions, lead to greater political and military independence among our current alliance partners. The emergence of these new centers of economic, political, and military power will result, at times, in a divergence of interests. This will increase our requirements for forces capable of responding unilaterally. Rising nationalism throughout the world will complicate further our ability to respond to threats to our worldwide interests. In the coming decade our access to overseas bases and overflight rights will continue to diminish which will place greater emphasis on the maintenance of sufficient strategic mobility assets and an increased premium on forces capable of operating and being sustained independent of overseas access.

The underdeveloped world's growing dissatisfaction over the gap between rich and poor nations will create a fertile breeding ground for insurgencies. These insurgencies have the potential to jeopardize regional stability and our access to vital economic and military resources. This situation will become more critical as our nation and allies, as well as potential adversaries, become more and more dependent on these strategic resources. If we are to have stability in these regions, maintain access to their resources, protect our citizens abroad, defend our vital installations, and deter conflict, we must maintain within our active force structure a credible military power projection capability with the flexibility to respond to conflict across the spectrum of violence throughout the globe.

Drug use and trafficking will continue to undermine both international and domestic stability. The widespread use of drugs has the potential to cause major damage to our economy and domestic social order. Our nation's demand for drugs contributes to the spread of narco-terrorism, and it is a contributing factor to insurgencies developing throughout the drug producing regions.

Domestic Environment

For the foreseeable future, it is unlikely that the defense budget environment will improve. Many of our citizens expect the changes in the Soviet threat to result in significant defense cost savings in both the short- and long-term. Growing concern with budget deficits will make it increasingly difficult to maintain the force structure needed to achieve our worldwide objectives. There will be little support for any military force structure that does not have aggregate utility across the spectrum of conflict The issue is clear. How do we provide for the adequate defense of our national interests with less available funding? solid business principles tell us to capitalize on complementary robustness, avoid unnecessary duplication and specialization, and increase the quality of our forces while reducing their quantity.

Although forward defense and coalition warfare will remain key components of our national security strategy, domestic support for overseas basing will continue to diminish unless our people are convinced of its utility and benefit. More importantly, if we are to maintain support for these bases, we must be able to show that our economically capable allies are shouldering their fair share of the cost burden of these bases.

It will be difficult to sustain support for overseas basing when bases in the United States are being evaluated for closure. In recent times, our citizens have shown a greater willingness to support action, including military action, when our interests have been threatened. This trend will probably continue, provided a link can be demonstrated between U.S. intervention and U.s. national interests. The challenge will be in articulating this link.

We must take the time to identify our interests and assess the threat. Once this is done, we can formulate a strategy and develop an affordable force structure that supports the achievement of our objectives at an acceptable level of risk.

Conclusion

Without question past and current developments in the Soviet Union and Eastern Europe require a reevaluation of our nation's security interests and requirements. At the same time, we also must recognize that there always will be social, economic, and political distinctions between nations. As long as these differences exist, nations will continue to take actions to advance their own self interests which will bring them into conflict with another nation's legitimate security concerns. Threats to our interests have and continue to exist separate from the Soviet Union. In fact, the majority of the crises we have responded to since the end of World War II have not directly involved the Soviet Union. This trend will continue.

The diverse nature of the threat and our national interests requires a flexible military force structure. The location of the threat, our interests, as well as our national character dictates that a significant portion of this capability be maritime in character. Our existing floating operating bases, warehouses, and airbases will have great utility as our overseas bases decrease and the requirement for independent action increases. There will be a requirement for a variety of forces to include amphibious forces, land and sea based prepositioned forces, airmobile, and airborne forces. The challenge will be to determine the correct mix based on need and affordability.

In the present era of uncertainty it is crucial that the United States remains a stable element. A contributing factor to stable world order is our capability to act decisively, if need be, in those instances where our interests are threatened. Unacceptable acts against the United States are not to be undertaken lightly and without risk by those who do not wish our nation well. If we are to continue to deter conflict at the lower spectrums of violence, we must maintain credible military and crisis response forces.

Reading and Reasoning

WHAT IS EDITORIAL BIAS?

This activity may be used as an individualized study guide for students in libraries and resource centers or as a discussion catalyst in small group and classroom discussion.

The capacity to recognize an author's point of view is an essential reading skill. The skill to read with insight and understanding involves the ability to detect different kinds of opinions or bias. *Sex bias, race bias, ethnocentric bias, political bias and religious bias* are five basic kinds of opinions expressed in editorials and all literature that attempts to persuade. They are briefly defined in the glossary below.

Glossary of Terms for Reading Skills

Sex Bias—the expression of dislike for and/or feeling of superiority over the opposite sex or a particular sexual minority

Race Bias—the expression of dislike for and/or feeling of superiority over a racial group

Ethnocentric Bias—the expression of a belief that one's own group, race, religion, culture or nation is superior. Ethnocentric persons judge others by their own standards and values.

Political Bias—the expression of political opinions and attitudes about domestic or foreign affairs

Religious Bias—the expression of a religious belief or attitude.

Guidelines

1. From the readings in Chapter Four, locate five sentences that provide examples of editorial opinion or bias.

2. Write down each of the above sentences and determine what kind of bias each sentence represents. Is it *sex bias, race bias, ethnocentric bias, political bias or religious bias?*

3. Make up one sentence statements that would be an example of each of the following: *sex bias, race bias, ethnocentric bias, political bias and religious bias.*

4. See if you can locate five sentences that are factual statements from the readings in Chapter Four.

BIBLIOGRAPHY

TRANSFORMING THE WARFARE STATE

A Cry for Capital: wanted—a new economic order. *World Press Review,* v. 38, June 1991: p.9-11.

A Thatcher-Reagan Legacy. *World Press Review*, v. 37, Dec. 1990: p.25.

Auster, B. B. A healthy military-industrial complex. *US News & World Report*, v. 108, Feb. 12, 1990: p.42-3.

Bacon, D. C. Closing a base opens doors. *Nation's Business,* v. 77, May 1989: p.9.

Barry, J. The coming cutbacks in military money. *Newsweek,* v. 117, Mar. 18, 1991: p.42-3.

Beers, D. Brother, can you spare $1.5 trillion. *Mother Jones*, v. 15, Jul./Aug. 1990: p.28-33.

Becker, S. Defense spending isn't stunting the U.S. economy. *Business Week,* Feb. 25, 1991: p.22.

Bernstein, C. Bush's other summit. *Time,* v. 136, Sept. 17, 1990: p.24.

Bischak, G. and Feldman, J. The Persian Gulf crisis: No retreat from conversion. *The New Economy,* v. 2, October 1990: p.1.

Borosage, R. How Bush kept the guns from turning to butter. *Rolling Stone*, Feb. 21, 1991: p.20-21.

Capitalist militarism impedes scientific progress. *The People,* March 11, 1989: p. 20-21.

China seeks aid from west in shift from military to commercial manufacture. *Aviation Week & Space Technology*, v. 131, Dec. 11, 1989: p.53.

Cooper J. Soviet military has a finger in every pie. *The Bulletin of the Atomic Scientists,* v. 46, Dec. 1990: p. 22-5.

Cortright, D. Shaping a peacetime economy. *The Progressive,* v. 53, Jan. 1989: p. 20-2.

Denny, J. Star struck. *Common Cause Magazine,* v. 17, Mar./April 1991: p.24-9.

Dwyer, P. Lessons from the front: the war against Iraq will change the way America arms itself. *Business Week*, Feb. 18, 1991: p.30-2.

Ellis, J. E. and Schine, E. Who pays for peace? *Business Week,* July 2, 1990: p.64-7.

Farrell, C. Why we should invest in human capital. *Business Week*, Dec. 17, 1990: p. 88-90.

Forbes, M. S. Greenlining our inner cities. *Forbes*, v. 146, July 9, 1990: 19-20.

Fuhrman, P. Ammo dump, anyone? *Forbes*, v. 146, Oct. 15, 1990: p.40-1.

Gerson, J. The quest for disarmament in a changing world. *The Nonviolent Activist*, Jan./Feb. 1989: p.3-6.

Greider, W. Protecting the Pentagon. *Utne Reader,* March/April 1991: p.108-9.

Gilmartin, P. A. Compromise defense bill preserves B-2. *Aviation Week & Space Technology,* v. 133, Oct. 22, 1990: p.23.

Gilmartin, P. A. Lower defense budgets forcing industry to boost productivity and reduce costs. *Aviation Week & Space Technology,* v. 134, Mar. 18, 1991: p.51-2.

Halberstam, D. Coming in from the Cold War. *The Washington Monthly,* v. 23, Jan./Feb. 1991: p.30-7.

Helprin, M. The one great lesson of the war. *The Wall Street Journal,* Feb. 26, 1991.

Javetski, B. How the crisis is scuttling the peace dividend. *Business Week*, Sept. 3, 1990: p.30-1.

Johnstone, D. Converts to conversion. *The Progressive*, v. 53, October 1989: p.14-15.

Kapstein, E. B. Effect of disarmament in the U.S.S.R.: From guns to butter. *Current*, v. 322, May 1990: p.25-9.

Keller, G. Toward a new defense policy. *Change,* V. 22, July/Aug. 1990: p.9.

Magdoff, H. A new economic bill of rights. *The Progressive,* V. 54, November 1990: p.32.

Magnuson, E. More billions for arms. *Time*, v. 137, April 8, 1991: p.28-9.

Mann, P. Bush administration will oppose defense industry conversion drive. *Aviation Week & Space Technology,* v. 133, August 6, 1990: p.20-1.

Mann, P. Preparing for a different world. *Aviation Week & Space Technology*, v. 130, Mar. 20, 1989: p.17.

Melman, S. and Dumas, L. J. Planning for economic

conversion. *The Nation,* v. 250, Apr. 16, 1990: p. 509.

Moran, T. H. International economics and national security. *Foreign Affairs,* v. 69, Winter 90/91: p.74-90.

Perry, N. J. How defense will change. *Fortune,* v. 123, Mar. 25, 1991: p.58.

Rinehart, D. From nuclear arms to candy and beer. *U.S. News & World Report,* v. 108, Feb. 19, 1990: p.50-1.

Sale, K. Conversion to what? *Utne Reader,* May/June 1990: p.46-7.

Sasser, J. R. Building a real peace economy. *USA Today* (periodical), v. 119, July 1990: p.56-7.

Saunders, N. C. Defense spending in the 1990s. *Monthly Labor Review,* v. 113, October 1990: p.15.

Smith, R. and Singer, D. American society in a global economy. *Society,* v. 28, Nov./Dec. 1990: p.66-71.

Stein, H. Peace dividends: what history teaches. *Current,* v. 324, July/Aug 1990: p.4-11.

The Arms race is still a menace. *The People,* Oct. 21, 1989: p.1.

Thorpe, N. Swords into plowshares. *World Press Review,* v. 38, Jan. 1991: p.58.

The stealth peace dividend. *Time,* v. 136, Nov. 5, 1990: p.30.

Vid, L. Guns into butter, Soviet style. *The Bulletin of the Atomic Scientists,* v. 46, Jan./Feb. 1990: p.16-20.

What should we defend? *The Defense Monitor,* v. 17, 1988: whole issue.